A Concise Guide to
Teaching Latin Literature

Oklahoma Series in Classical Culture

A CONCISE GUIDE TO
TEACHING LATIN LITERATURE

EDITED BY
Ronnie Ancona

UNIVERSITY OF OKLAHOMA PRESS : NORMAN

Also by Ronnie Ancona

Time and the Erotic in Horace's Odes (Durham, N.C., 1994)
Horace: Selected Odes and Satire 1.9 (Wauconda, Ill., 1999, 2005)
Writing Passion: A Catullus Reader (Wauconda, Ill., 2004)
(ed., with Ellen Greene) *Gendered Dynamics in Latin Love Poetry* (Baltimore, Md., 2005)
(with David Murphy) *A Horace Workbook* (Wauconda, Ill., 2005)

Library of Congress Cataloging-in-Publication Data

A concise guide to teaching Latin literature / edited by Ronnie Ancona.
    p.   cm. — (Oklahoma series in classical culture)
   ISBN-13: 978-0-8061-3797-1 (pbk. : alk. paper)
   ISBN-10: 0-8061-3797-5
   1. Latin literature—Study and teaching. 2. Latin literature—History and criticism. I. Ancona, Ronnie, 1951–.

PA2063.C56 2007
870.71—dc22

2006025580

A Concise Guide to Teaching Latin Literature is Volume 32 in the Oklahoma Series in Classical Culture.

The paper in this book meets the guidelines for permanence and durability of the Committee on Production Guidelines for Book Longevity of the Council on Library Resources, Inc. ∞

1 2 3 4 5 6 7 8 9 10

discipulis meis

CONTENTS

INTRODUCTION

Ronnie Ancona

This book is devoted to showing how an awareness of current scholarly debates can enhance the teaching of major Latin authors, especially at the advanced high school level and the intermediate and advanced undergraduate levels. It has been my experience during many years of teaching and contact with other teachers at both the college and secondary levels that teachers are far more interested in scholarship and its possible pedagogical uses than is often assumed. The interest is always there; however, the time too often is not. For college faculty, there is understandable pressure to remain current in one's area of specialization and research, which may or may not coincide with one's teaching areas. For secondary school faculty, the teaching day is much longer, and competing interests and commitments include, but are not limited to, extracurricular responsibilities and professional growth and training specifically related to adolescence education. Given these time constraints, many teachers at both levels frequently teach Latin authors about whom they have had little time to do extra reading in current scholarship. An overview of recent scholarship on major Latin authors is needed for pedagogical purposes, and it is in recognition of this need that this book was written.

The chapters address Catullus, Ovid, Horace, Cicero, and Vergil, authors commonly taught at both the college level and the secondary school level. These five are the Advanced Placement Program Latin authors (Vergil for the Vergil Examination and Catullus, combined with Cicero, Horace, or Ovid, for the Latin Literature Examination). Each contributor to this book is a Latin scholar teaching at the college level who has written a scholarly book on the author he or she addresses here. Most of them have also had extensive contact with secondary school teachers, through such activities as teacher training programs, Advanced Placement Latin Examination grading, National Endowment for the Humanities workshops, and textbook writing.

Each chapter addresses aspects of current scholarship on its subject author as well as how that scholarship might affect teaching. The individual contributions raise a number of general issues as well as show how those play out with regard to particular Latin selections. It is my hope that teachers will find it useful that the theoretical material is addressed in the context of specific passages they might use with their own students. The book can be browsed through or read from beginning to end, or selected chapters can be read in isolation. Some teachers may prefer to single out the chapters on particular authors about whom they want further material for the classroom, while others may prefer to read first about some recent scholarly developments in relation to authors not part of their current teaching. This is not intended as a "how to" book, but rather as one that will be suggestive and exploratory. Each teacher will decide what portions of the book might be adapted for classroom use and how.

All of the chapters, in one way or another, will show that there are many and varied ways to approach the reading and study of Catullus, Ovid, Horace, Cicero, and Vergil. The one feature common to all is an attempt to demonstrate the excitement for reader, teacher, and student of engaging with new scholarship on a particular Latin author. Each of the contributors has staked out a scholarly position on the author that he or she examines; the purpose of these essays, however, is not to further those specific arguments, but rather to draw upon the contributors' scholarly expertise in order to highlight significant aspects of current scholarly inquiry on these five major Latin authors.[1]

William Fitzgerald's chapter, "Catullus, the Collection: Poems, Contexts, and Subjectivity," proceeds from the notion that how one interprets a particular poem of Catullus will depend on the context of the other poems within which it is read. Taking Poems 11 and 51 as his starting point, Fitzgerald shows how they can be read as something other than the end and beginning of a love affair. Using key concepts in current Catullan criticism— such as subjectivity, performativity, and homosocial bonding— he shows that other poems in the collection can destabilize our understanding of a particular poem. For example, the simultaneity of love and hate in Poem 85 can affect assumptions about the beginning and ending of an affair, while neighboring poems, such as 10 and 50, provide contexts that encourage reinterpretation of both Poems 11 and 51. Fitzgerald takes familiar material from Catullus and shows how it can be seen anew in light of recent critical discussions in Catullan scholarship.

Barbara Weiden Boyd's chapter, "A Poet Restored: Contemporary Scholarship and the Teaching of Ovid," continues Fitzgerald's interest in the reader, and his or her choices, as central to interpretation. Whereas Fitzgerald's focus is on how the reading of other poems of Catullus might affect our reading of a particular poem, Boyd's is on how Ovid himself invites the reader to interpret his work in varied ways. Using as examples *Amores* 1.9, with its image of love/war, and a selection from the *Fasti* featuring Romulus/Augustus, Boyd shows how Ovid forces his readers through pointed oppositional perspectives to be active participants in the construction of meaning. In addition, she uses the metaphor of "exile" to discuss the place Ovid has had (or not had) in the classroom in recent years. She concludes that changes in the critical reception of Ovid—including a renewed valuing of his work as far from second-rate—have gone hand in hand with the reintroduction of more Ovid into the secondary school and college classroom.

Ronnie Ancona's chapter, "'Tensile Horace': Negotiating Critical Boundaries," continues Boyd's interest in revaluing a poet's work by arguing that Horace, if seen as other than the dry, emotionless giver of advice he has sometimes been characterized as, can be far more interesting to the Latin student. Focusing on the "tensile" quality of Horace's poetry that allows it to "stretch" in different directions, Ancona discusses several key notions in current Horatian scholarship that address in one way or another Horace's almost uncanny ability not to be categorized. Using *Odes* 1.37, the Cleopatra Ode, as an example, Ancona takes ideas emerging from recent books on Horace to show how this particular poem can be seen from the following critical perspectives: the genre of lyric as "political negotiator," the importance of "face" in relation to deference and authority, the centrality of "conditionality" for a poet negotiating in the arena of praise, the gendered status of power and desire, and the importance of a "gift economy" to Horace's actions and poetics. Ancona shows how one particularly well-known poem can be the starting point for discussion of several now critical ideas in recent scholarship on Horace.

James M. May's chapter, "Ciceronian Scholarship in the Latin Classroom," focuses on the purpose of Ciceronian rhetoric and its place in the larger Roman historical context. Just as politics is central to Horace's Cleopatra Ode, so is Cicero's own political career central to the creation and performance of his rhetoric. Using as examples *Pro Archia, In Catilinam 1,* and *Pro Caelio,* May explores a wide variety of current approaches to Cicero's rhetoric, focusing in particular on "persuasive-process criticism," which views a speech as "the record of an oral process, aimed at persuading a particular audience in the context of a particular set of circumstances." Bringing together issues of audience manipulation and the relation between orator and jury, the use of digressions in speeches, and the portrayal by Cicero of his own

character and the character of others, May shows how the identification of a particular rhetorical challenge has far-reaching
explanatory value.

The final chapter, "Dido in Translation," by Richard F. Thomas,
is a discussion of a particular variety of reception study, namely
translation. Taking as his focus the judgment of Aeneas' treatment of Dido in the *Aeneid,* an issue about which generations of
students and teachers, as well as scholars, have argued, Thomas
shows how the act of translating—which of course is the province of both published translators and students alike—is part
of a larger project of reception: interpreting an earlier, original
text. Discussing words such as *culpa* (fault, flaw, slip?) that are
difficult to translate from Latin, Thomas shows how translations
from Chaucer, Dryden, and less well-known figures such as
John Davis Long can be used to show that translation is part of
the ongoing interpretive process and that it can lead us back in
rewarding ways to our original texts. Thomas' chapter is perhaps
a fitting conclusion for a book that attempts to show how scholarship and pedagogy can be linked, for it is an example of
Vergilian scholarship about translation, and translation is an
activity that serves as a pedagogical tool in any Latin classroom.

A few words of background: This volume is a direct result
of the American Philological Association's recently expanded
mission of serving the interests of classicists at all levels of
teaching and education. In 2003, at the APA Annual Meeting in
New Orleans, the APA Education Committee and the Joint APA/
American Classical League Committee on Classics in American
Education sponsored "Latin Scholarship/Latin Pedagogy: Scholars
Address the Classroom," the first of a planned series of panels
the purpose of which is to forge a link between scholars and
teachers at both the college and the secondary school levels—
two groups whose interests are more closely aligned than is
sometimes acknowledged. I was the panel organizer. The enthusiasm with which the panel was received led to interest in its
publication. This volume contains in expanded and revised form

the five papers that were delivered at that session. I would like to thank Elizabeth Keitel, then APA Vice President for Education; Adam Blistein, APA Executive Director; Minna Duchovnay, then APA Coordinator, Meetings, Program, and Administration; and the APA Program Committee in 2003 for their support in making the original panel a success, including scheduling it at a time that was convenient for teachers at all levels and publicizing it to teachers in the greater New Orleans area.

John Drayton, Director and Classics Acquisitions Editor of the University of Oklahoma Press, led me to see that our panel was of interest to a wider audience, and for this I am grateful. He and his assistants, Brian Benson and, later, Astrud Reed, made the publishing experience an easy and pleasant one. Ward Briggs, who was Series Editor at the time for the Oklahoma Series in Classical Culture, helped to guide the manuscript to the Press; Alice Stanton, Managing Editor, and Jane Lyle, free-lance copyeditor, gave it careful attention in its final stages. The anonymous readers for the Press provided helpful comments. Steven Cole offered computer assistance and, along with David Ancona-Cole, an environment both conducive to work and a welcome relief from it.

The conversation between secondary-level teachers and college teachers, and further between "teachers" and "scholars" (for, of course, these roles we take on are not mutually exclusive), must be an ongoing and continuous one. This volume's focus on scholarship and the classroom is intended as one contribution to that dialogue.

NOTE

1. For a recent overview of studying and teaching Latin literature today, see the introductory remarks by Lowell Edmunds in "Critical Divergences: New Directions in the Study and Teaching of Roman Literature," *Transactions and Proceedings of the American Philological*

Association 135 (2005): 1–13, and the papers that follow in the same volume, all derived from a conference held at Rutgers University in 2003. The focus of that set of papers is what issues Latin scholars are currently pursuing and why. In contrast, this book seeks to take just a few such issues in the context of five major authors and show how they can be incorporated into the college and secondary school classroom.

A CONCISE GUIDE TO
TEACHING LATIN LITERATURE

CHAPTER 1

CATULLUS, THE COLLECTION
Poems, Contexts, and Subjectivity

William Fitzgerald

There are some ancient authors who seem appropriately remote from our world, challenging us to make a leap of the imagination into a different set of norms, assumptions, or aesthetic values— Aeschylus and Pindar on the exciting end, but also more sedate poets, such as Horace. By contrast, we have Catullus, "our" Catullus, the passionate rebel whom we seem to know already, and that can be a problem if we ask of history that it take us somewhere else, or at least remind us that ours is not the only possible, or even plausible, world. But perhaps all is not as it seems; perhaps Catullus falls into the category of the "false friend," a term used by teachers of modern languages for a foreign word that looks familiar but means something quite different from the English word it resembles. If you are speaking German, for instance, *Gift* means "poison." One area in which what we already know is likely to lead us astray once we enter the ancient world is the sexual, but I will not address that topic, because Paul Allen Miller has already written an excellent introduction to teaching Catullus (and thinking differently) on sex.[1] In that area, as in others, Catullus is so near and yet so far, as Peter Wiseman warns us in the opening of his book *Catullus and His World,* where he makes a vivid case that first-century B.C. Rome is more alien than we sometimes think.[2]

3

In what follows, I am going to suggest some ways in which Catullus' love poetry may not be quite what it has seemed. But it is not the love poetry per se that is my focus. What I want to discuss is the Catullus we construct out of the extraordinarily varied collection that has come down under his name. Not surprisingly, Catullus has the reputation of being a man of oppositions— tender and violent (sometimes in the same poem); trivial and profound; playful and serious (even sanctimonious); learned and colloquial; Transpadane provincial and Roman sophisticate. The poems themselves, as Selden (1992) has reminded us, can be simultaneously transparent and opaque, and a given poem may allow two quite contradictory but equally plausible readings. Faced with the sheer variety of this collection, we tend to look for a center of gravity (the *real* Catullus); we try to distinguish the central from the peripheral and to decide what is to be read from which perspective. And we are encouraged to do so: themes and persons recur, and the collection seems to tease us with the ghost of a narrative, the impression that it might add up. It is like a Rorschach test that reads *us* rather than vice versa.

Not surprisingly, the interpretation of Catullus, who has come to represent lyric subjectivity par excellence, has been affected by the rethinking of subjectivity that has been at the center of the postmodern turn.[3] Instead of imagining the self as an inner core that undergoes, accumulates, and is changed by experience, modern and postmodern thinking has understood the self or subject more as a position within a given structure. To be a speaking subject, for instance, we need to adopt the position of the first person, sited by oppositions and relations to the second (you) and third (he/she/it) persons respectively. The self within the family is a position defined by prescribed and proscribed relations to mother, father, brother, and sister. In the political sphere, the subject learns to speak from within the ideology of a class. And so on. The accumulation of heterogeneous, overlapping, or interrelated structures within which we must take up the position of subject makes the self more like a switchboard than an inner core. The contemporary reader of Catullus' collection will be more interested in seeing how a particular poem may change depending on what poems one relates it to than in locating a core repertoire of the *real* Catullus, in relation to which the other poems range in a descending scale of seriousness.[4] Paul Allen Miller, who credits Catullus with the invention of a lyric consciousness, has this to say about the collection: "each poem of Catullus can fit into a variety of narratives, no one of which is necessarily the single correct one, but all of which have as their center the projection of an ego which exists in and between the individual poems themselves, and which is the true ground of all these potential narratives. The ego is not the historical Catullus, but rather is a function of the reader's engagement with the collection" (1994, 74–75).

I will now take two poems and show, very sketchily, some of the different connections they might make. My poems are cc. 11 and 51, the translation of Sappho and the bitter farewell to Lesbia (assuming that she is the addressee) which Catullus entrusts to Furius and Aurelius. Kenneth Quinn, in his excellent commentary, voices what used to be a common opinion when he says that these clearly mark the beginning and the end of the Lesbia affair. These are the only two poems in the Catullan corpus in the Sapphic stanza, and the unusual word *identidem* occurs in both of them and nowhere else: at 51.3, the man who "again and again" gazes at and listens to Lesbia is a god; at 11.19, Lesbia embraces her three hundred lovers and "again and again" exhausts their loins (*ilia rumpens*). With the Sappho translation, so the story goes, Catullus introduces the pseudonym Lesbia for his lover Clodia, associating her with the charm and sophistication of the Greek poet while applying Sappho's symptoms of love to his own experience.

> Ille mi par esse deo videtur,
> ille, si fas est, superare divos,
> qui sedens adversus identidem te,
>   spectat et audit

dulce ridentem, misero quod omnis
eripit sensus mihi: nam simul te,
Lesbia, aspexi, nihil est super mi
• • •
lingua sed torpet, tenuis sub artus
flamma demanat, sonitu suopte
tintinant aures, gemina teguntur
    lumina nocte.
otium, Catulle, tibi molestum est:
otio exsultas, nimiumque gestis:
otium et reges prius et beatas
    perdidit urbes.

That man seems to me the equal of a god; that man, if it is right
to say so, seems to outdo the gods, who sitting across from you
again and again sees and hears you laughing sweetly—a thing
which steals the senses from lovesick me. For as soon as I catch
sight of you, Lesbia, I have nothing left . . . but my tongue sticks,
a slender flame spreads through my limbs, my ears ring with their
own sound, and my eyes are covered by a double night. Idleness,
Catullus, is a nuisance to you; in idleness you exult too much and
become excitable; idleness has destroyed kings and rich cities
in the past.[5]

Poem 11, whose final image of a flower cut by the plow
alludes to a wedding poem of Sappho (Fr. 105c), then closes
the affair.

Furi et Aureli, comites Catulli
sive in extremos penetrabit Indos,
litus ut longe resonante Eoa
    tunditur unda,
sive in Hyrcanos Arabasve molles,
seu Sagas sagittiferosque Parthos,
sive quae septemgeminus colorat
    aequora Nilus,

sive trans altas gradietur Alpes,
Caesaris visens monimenta magni,
Gallicum Rhenum horribilesque ulti-
    mosque Britannos,
omnia haec, quaecumque feret voluntas
caelitum, temptare simul parati,
pauca nuntiate meae puellae
    non bona dicta.
cum suis vivat valeatque moechis,
quos simul complexa tenet trecentos,
nullum amans vere sed identidem omnium
    ilia rumpens:
nec meum respectet, ut ante, amorem,
qui illius culpa cecidit velut prati
ultimi flos, praetereunte postquam
    tactus aratro est.

Furius and Aurelius—Catullus' companions, whether he reaches
the furthest India, whose shore is echoing all its length to the
crashing eastern wave, or the soft Arabs or the Hyrcani, or the
Sagae or the Parthians who fight with bows, or the lands which
the seven-mouthed Nile, overflowing, colors, or whether he strides
across the high Alps, viewing the monuments of great Caesar, the
Gallic Rhine, or the terrifying Britons at earth's end—prepared as
you are to attempt with me all this, whatever the will of the gods
commands, pass on these none too pleasant words to my girl: let
her live and flourish with her adulterers whom she embraces three
hundred at a time, truly loving none, but again and again breaking
their manhood; and let him not look to my love, as before, which
has fallen by her fault like the flower on the edge of the field,
touched by the passing plow.

One way to read the Lesbia poems is to plot their location
between these two points in what has been dubbed "the novel of
Catullus." The collection becomes the story of a love affair
reconstructed in the form of the archetypal modern genre, the

novel. It moves from infatuation to hatred, via disillusionment.[6] But in the case of cc. 11 and 51, the Catullan collection as we have it reverses the order of these events, if that is what they are. Although we do not, and without further information *cannot,* know whether Catullus ordered the collection as we have it, this reversal of narrative order might prompt us to try another tack. Suppose we abandon the narrative model and take another very famous poem of Catullus as the prism through which to see cc. 11 and 51:

> Odi et amo: quare id faciam, fortasse requiris,
> nescio, sed fieri sentio et excrucior. (c. 85)

> I hate and I love: if perhaps you ask me why, I don't know, but I
> feel it and it tortures me.

Here love and hate are simultaneous, not the beginning and the end. From this perspective, the collection's reversal of the narrative order of 11 and 51 (in a story that moves from passionate infatuation to disillusionment) might suggest that Catullus bounces repetitively (*identidem*) between these two positions: woman as goddess and woman as whore, to put it crudely. Micaela Janan puts it more subtly in her Lacanian reading of Catullus, *When the Lamp Is Shattered.*[7] It is characteristic of contemporary criticism to replace narrative explications, where one thing changes into another because of contingent factors, such as Lesbia's faithlessness, with readings that look for an underlying contradiction or paradox. For Janan, the relation between these two poems is symptomatic of subjectivity in general, which is intrinsically divided in itself; human subjects, according to Lacan, are constituted in the desire to achieve a wholeness that is impossible, given that subjectivity is always implicated in structures that preexist the self and that it depends partially on recognition by others. Woman is fantasized by Man as the complement that will heal this split in his subjectivity, but to no avail. Since this fantasy is just that, and doomed to failure, Man must find reasons for this failure that put the blame on Woman. Catullus' cc. 11 and 51 are the two poles of the impossibility of Man finding his complement in Woman. If these poems are paired by meter and represent the extremes of Catullus' relationship with Lesbia, then it is noteworthy that both ecstatic love and disillusionment are expressed in images of bodily assault, and this in spite of the fact that Catullus attempts to screen himself from Lesbia by interposing others (the man speaking to Lesbia in c. 51 and Furius and Aurelius in c. 11). The heedless plow of c. 11 is really another form of the erotic power that causes the gazing speaker of c. 51 to disintegrate in the sight of his beloved. In c. 51, *identidem* ("*again and again* hears and sees you laughing sweetly") reflects the fascination of the distant, godlike Lesbia, in whose contemplation the subject disintegrates; in 11, *identidem* ("but *again and again* breaking their manhood") expresses the omnivorousness of Lesbia's sexuality. Whether as object of worship or as whore, Lesbia is for everybody and therefore not really for anybody, least of all Catullus. *Odi et amo* can be taken as an emblem of the collection not because Catullus is a man who, at various times, loves (c. 51) or hates (c. 11), but because love and hate in their extreme forms respond to two versions of the unattainable Woman: the goddess and the whore.

So we can read the connection between these two poems as a narrative development or a paradoxical circularity. But let us now look at each in its immediate context in the collection. Next to c. 11 is a disarming little anecdote about two men and a woman (c. 10). C. 11 is also triangular, and gets to Lesbia only in the last two stanzas, the rest being addressed to Furius and Aurelius.[8] The edge of the field in the final stanza of c. 11 contrasts sharply with the grandiose geographical perspectives of the opening, perspectives that have an imperial scope. One of the reasons for believing 11 to come late in the affair, indeed in Catullus' life, is the reference to Caesar's conquests of 55 B.C.

in line 10 (*Caesaris visens monimenta magni*). The imperial theme features also in the previous poem (c. 10), for the anecdote told by Catullus centers around his report on the time he spent in the entourage of the governor of Bithynia, Memmius. In c. 10, Catullus is the butt of his own anecdote, but the immediate source of his discomfiture is a woman, the new girlfriend of his friend Varus, who picks up Catullus idling in the forum and takes him to meet her.

Varus me meus ad suos amores
visum duxerat e foro otiosum,
scortillum, ut mihi tum repente visum est,
non sane illepidum neque invenustum.
huc ut venimus, incidere nobis
sermones varii, in quibus, quid esset
iam Bithynia, quo modo se haberet,
et quonam mihi profuisset aere.
respondi id quod erat, nihil neque ipsis
nec praetoribus esse nec cohorti,
cur quisquam caput unctius referret,
praesertim quibus esset irrumator
praetor, nec faceret pili cohortem.
"at certe tamen," inquiunt "quod illic
natum dicitur esse, comparasti
ad lecticam homines." ego, ut puellae
unum me facerem beatiorem,
"non" inquam "mihi tam fuit maligne,
ut, provincia quod mala incidisset
non possem octo homines parare rectos."
at mi nullus erat neque hic neque illic
fractum qui veteris pedem grabati
in collo sibi collocare posset.
hic illa, ut decuit cinaediorem,
"quaeso," inquit "mihi, mi Catulle, paulum,
istos commoda: nam volo ad Serapim
deferri." "mane" inquii puellae,

"istud quod modo dixeram me habere,
fugit me ratio: meus sodalis—
Cinna est Gaius—is sibi paravit.
verum, utrum illius an mei, quid ad me?
utor tam bene quam mihi pararim.
sed tu insulsa male et molesta vivis,
per quam non licet esse neglegentem."

My friend Varus took me to the forum, as I idled there, to meet
his girlfriend; a little whore, I noticed on the spot, but not without
charm or beauty. When we got here, various subjects came up,
among which, what was the news from Bithynia now and how it
was doing, and what sort of profit I had made there. I answered
with the truth: there was nothing for the natives, or the praetors or
their staff, no reason to come back slicker than one had set out,
especially for those whose praetor screwed them over and didn't
give a damn for his staff. "But surely," they said, "you obtained
for yourself some litterbearers; we're told it's the local product."
I, wanting to make myself seem uniquely fortunate to the girl,
said, "Things weren't so bad; just because I drew a bad province
doesn't mean I couldn't scrape up eight stout men." In fact, I had
no one, neither here nor there, who could shoulder the burden of
an old cot's broken leg. At which she said (just like her, the cow),
"Please, Catullus my friend, let me borrow them a while; I need
to ride to Serapis' temple." "Hold on," I said to her, "when I told
you I *had* them, well, I forgot: my friend Cinna (Gaius Cinna, I
mean), *he's* the one who bought them. But, whether his or mine,
who cares? I use them as though I'd bought them myself. But
you, you're a bore and a drag to have around if a man can't be
careless with his talk."

This urbane anecdote may seem far removed from the ago-
nized world of c. 11, but the two poems have much in common
once we look past the difference in emotional temperature: in both
cases, a woman victimizes Catullus; in both cases, she enters
the scene in the context of a relationship between men, and the

relationships between the characters are in both cases played out against the backdrop of Roman imperialism. In *Catullan Provocations,* I argue that there is a relation between the pseudo-urbane carelessness of Catullus' lie in c. 10 and the indifferent heedlessness of Lesbia embracing her three hundred lovers in c. 11, and that both of these forms of *neglegentia* are connected to an imperial ethos that underwrites loose talk in the metropolis.[9] Furius and Aurelius can casually promise to accompany Catullus across the Alps in the wake of Caesar's conquests, and Catullus can casually lie about the slaves he has picked up while accompanying the governor of Bithynia. Both poems have an imperial agenda, and the love of Catullus for Lesbia takes place within an imperial world, not in an isolated idyll, as cc. 5 and 7 might suggest to modern readers.

In the end, of course, the Catullus who tells us the anecdote against himself in c. 10 is master of the situation, and he emphasizes the power of poetry to make something out of nothing in lines 20–22 (*at mi nullus erat neque hic neque illic . . .*). Similarly in the final stanzas of 11, where the heedless plow slices the flower of Catullus' love, the *poet* Catullus very precisely and deliberately sculpts his work of art, appropriating the brutality of Lesbia's plow to accomplish the Sapphic stanza's form, which closes with a final short line. If we distinguish the poet from the lover in c. 11, and the Catullus who recounts the anecdote in c. 10 from the Catullus who is discomfited within it, then we can see that the victimization of the one serves to display the mastery of the other. Reading these poems together produces a different agenda from the one that emerges if we pursue the connection between 11 and 51 as moments in Catullus' affair with Lesbia. To begin with, the two poems both attempt to situate the power of Catullus the poet by using the victimization of Catullus the lover as (broadly speaking) a foil to show off the poet's mastery. In this light, c. 11 is not so much the anguished self-expression of a tormented lover as a *performance* of poetic mastery, and here I am introducing an important term in contemporary treatments

of Catullus, and of Roman culture in general: in fact, one could
say that "performance" now plays the role that "self-expression"
did for earlier generations, as the most general term for what
Catullus' poetry does.[10] Poetry as self-expression is the poet's
attempt to communicate adequately what has been felt, but many
scholars believe that in the Roman context (and not only there)
it is more appropriate to think of poetry as an attempt to display
mastery of the word in a competitive context: a man must establish or prove what he is, against those who makes similar claims,
by means of a commanding performance. In Roman elite male
society, mastery depended to a great extent on verbal performance,
most notably, of course, oratorical. Krostenko (2001) has shown
that the distinctive terms of approval in the Catullan collection
(*bellus, urbanus, lepidus, venustus,* and the like) should be seen
in the context of new kinds of competitive social performance that
flourished in the last two generations of the republic. Catullus'
conspicuous displays of urbanity (on which see Fitzgerald 1995,
87–113) would be a prime example of this kind of performance,
and c. 10 is a supremely urbane performance in which Catullus
tells a story featuring himself as the butt of the joke, thereby
proving that he is beyond, or above, social embarrassment.

In the intensely competitive world of elite Roman society,
the most important currency was masculinity, and David Wray
argues, in his *Catullus and the Poetics of Roman Manhood,* that
what is being performed in Catullus' poetry is manhood. This is
most obviously the case for Catullus' insults threatening a phallic
aggression that will establish once and for all who is the man
(c. 16, for instance). But how do we explain in these terms the
provocative effeminacy of so much Catullan poetry, which, Catullus himself tells us, needs to be "a bit soft and not quite straight"
(*molliculi et parum pudici,* c. 16.8) in order to have its effect?
An elite Roman male of Catullus' time was required to be both
masculine and sophisticated, and this demanded that his social
performance walk the tightrope between too much virility (veering
toward rusticity) and too little (skirting effeminacy). As a result,

he was always vulnerable to one charge or the other. As Wray puts it, "There was no comfort zone at the center in which he could be certain of being sufficiently cultivated without exposing himself to accusations of effeminacy, or of being sufficiently rough-hewn without incurring the charge of rusticity" (2001, 208). Catullus' solution was to occupy at one time or another both the hypermasculine and the provocatively effeminate stance, in each case leaving the interlocutor, and indeed the reader, gasping for breath at his audacity. It no longer matters *how* he is performing, since the very power of the performance itself becomes a form of masculine self-assertion, proving, as did c. 10, that Catullus is beyond the reach of the social anxiety under which any Roman male might be expected to suffer, given what was demanded of him. Where our instinct may be to turn away in disgust from what we see as a particularly compromising self-revelation, it may be more appropriate to think of ourselves as targets of a provocation.

Another similarity between cc. 10 and 11 takes us in a different direction. Love poetry, we tend to think, centers on two people. But if we look more closely, many of the love scenarios in Catullus are triangles rather than duos. In cc. 5 and 7, for instance, the disapproving and the jealous busybodies are an essential component in the dramatis personae of Catullus' love. In c. 10 Varus needs to show off his girl to his friend Catullus, and in c. 11 Catullus insults (or jokes with) Furius and Aurelius, who are cast as go-betweens for his message to Lesbia. Putting the Lesbia affair, with its familiar romantic scenario, at the center of the collection, and of Catullus' subjectivity, means relegating the other men addressed in these poems to the periphery—where they look on, interfering or intervening as rivals. But recent study of the heterosexual romantic tradition in European literature has shifted the focus from men and women to cast the primary relationship as one between men, who "traffic in women" as they communicate with each other.[11] Men formed alliances and mutually enhanced one another's status at the same time that they competed fiercely for office and cultural prestige. With the notable

exception of Lesbia, Catullus' world is mostly one of relations
between men. A good example of this is c. 50, and we will see that c. 51,
like c. 11, also looks different if we consider it in its immediate
context in the collection, as David Wray has done (2001, 88–109),
although he was not the first to do so. Poem 50 is a playful letter
to the poet C. Licinius Calvus, and like the Sappho translation,
it describes the physical symptoms of love, only here they are
occasioned by a day of shared poetic activity between two men.

Hesterno, Licini, die otiosi
multum lusimus in meis tabellis,
ut convenerat esse delicatos:
scribens versiculos uterque nostrum
ludebat numero modo hoc modo illoc,
reddens mutua per iocum atque vinum.
atque illinc abii tuo lepore
incensus, Licini, facetiisque,
ut nec me miserum cibus iuvaret
nec somnus tegeret quiete ocellos,
sed toto indomitus furore lecto
versarer, cupiens videre lucem,
ut tecum loquerer simulque ut essem.
at defessa labore membra postquam
semimortua lectulo iacebant,
hoc, iucunde, tibi poema feci,
ex quo perspiceres meum dolorem.
nunc audax cave sis, precesque nostras,
oramus, cave despuas, ocelle,
ne poenas Nemesis reposcat a te.
est vemens dea: laedere hanc caveto.

Yesterday, Licinius, at our ease, we played a lot in my notebooks,
as we had agreed to be frivolous: playing in this meter, then in
that, swapping verses, joking, drinking. And I left you, Licinius,
inflamed with your charm and witticisms, so that I could not eat

(poor me)! But tossed all over the bed, my passion uncontrolled, longing to see the light of day, so that I could speak and be with you. But when my limbs, worn out with toil, were lying on the bed, half-dead, I made this poem for you, my friend, that you might understand my suffering. Now see you don't get bold; I beg you, dear, not to reject my prayers lest Nemesis exact a penalty from you. She's an imperious goddess; don't provoke her!

Wray points out that, taken as a unit, cc. 50 and 51 begin and end with the concept of *otium*. More significantly, together they would replicate the relation between cc. 65 and 66, in which a letter to a friend, apologizing for not sending the poems that the friend had requested (c. 65), offers as a substitute the poem that follows (c. 66), a translation of the Hellenistic poet Callimachus. In cc. 50 and 51, Wray sees another pairing of a covering letter with a Greek poem that Catullus has translated into Latin; when Catullus says, "hoc, iucunde, tibi poema feci" (16), he may be referring to c. 51, not c. 50. The love language of the Sappho translation that follows would echo the outrageous language that Catullus had used in describing the impression made on him by Calvus' charm. These poems, according to Wray, fit into a genre of Catullan epistles to men (compare also c. 30 and c. 38), epistles that provocatively take the form of a lover's complaint in order to issue a challenge inviting the addressee to reciprocate with a comparable performance.[12] In this context, the apparent bathos of the final stanza, where Catullus veers away from the symptoms of love to an ironic self-address, may be less striking, and in this stanza we may hear the voice of an imagined response from Calvus.

What you see in a given Catullan poem, then, depends to a large extent on what connections you make with other poems in the oeuvre. Experiments of the sort I have been making are a useful critical or pedagogical practice. They make us aware of the categories and narratives that we *want* to find, and they help to open us to different possibilities. We have instinctive and deep-rooted feelings about the different "levels of intent" of the Catullan corpus, about what is serious or deeply felt and what is mere play. But our instincts are formed in a context very different from Catullus'. When Catullus rejects the judgment of "stern old men" (*senum severiorum,* c. 5.2) and others who may take a critical interest in his love, he is not necessarily imagining the kind of private idyll that is familiar to our own romantic ideals, in which value is located in privacy and feeling. In the Roman context, it is more likely that Catullus is making a move within the public world of men competing and allying with other men.

On a broader level, the kind of experiment in multiple contexts that I have pursued shows how different agendas fit together, or at least overlay each other. It is not necessary to say, for instance, that c. 11 is *either* Catullus' impassioned and bitter farewell to Lesbia *or* a poem about empire and male bonding. The locating of a particular poem in multiple contexts corresponds to contemporary ideas about how our subjectivities are constituted. Instead of a solid and radiating center of consciousness, the subject is compounded of its positions within a multiplicity of heterogeneous but interconnected structures, preexisting the individual who assumes a position within them. Catullus is both familiar and strange to us as the postmodern subject is to itself.

NOTES

1. Focusing on Catullus 16, Miller seeks to show how Catullus helps students to think differently about "(1) the historical mutability of socially acceptable behavior; (2) the constructed nature of sexual identity; (3) the nature and function of gender; (4) the omnipresence and play of both power and resistance; and (5) the admonitory and optative function of poetic art" (2000, 37).

2. Wiseman 1985, 4–14, focusing on cruelty and on sexual mores.

3. A good short introduction to modern theory is Culler 1997. Chapter 8 provides a useful account of new thinking on subjectivity.

4. The theory of "levels of intent" was first advanced by Quinn 1959, 27–43, which remains a classic of Catullan interpretation.

5. All translations are my own.

6. On "the novel of Catullus" in modern scholarship, see Fitzgerald 1995, 26–29, and for modern novels on Catullus, 211–35.

7. Janan 1994, 66–76.

8. Poems 15, 16, 21, 23, 24, and 26 suggest that Furius and Aurelius were enemies and that this opening is ironic.

9. Fitzgerald 1995, 183–84.

10. Selden 1992 and Krostenko 2001 both relate Catullan performance to the broader Roman context.

11. See Sedgwick 1985, who relates her concept of "homosocial desire" to Rene Girard's theory of "mimetic desire" and to Claude Lévi-Strauss' "traffic in women."

12. Wray 2001, 96–109.

REFERENCES

Culler, Jonathan. 1997. *Literary Theory: A Very Short Introduction.* Oxford: Oxford University Press.

Fitzgerald, William. 1995. *Catullan Provocations: Lyric Poetry and the Drama of Position.* Berkeley: University of California Press.

Janan, Micaela. 1994. *"When the Lamp Is Shattered": Desire and Narrative in Catullus.* Carbondale: Southern Illinois University Press.

Krostenko, Brian. 2001. *Cicero, Catullus, and the Language of Social Performance.* Chicago: University of Chicago Press.

Miller, Paul Allen. 1994. *Lyric Texts and Lyric Consciousness: The Birth of a Genre from Archaic Greece to Augustan Rome.* London: Routledge.

———. 2000. "Reading Catullus, Thinking Differently." *Helios* 27 (2000): 33–52.

Putnam, Michael. 1974. "Catullus 11: The Ironies of Integrity." *Ramus* 3 (1974): 70–86.

Quinn, Kenneth. 1959. *The Catullan Revolution.* Melbourne: Melbourne University Press.

Sedgwick, Eve Kosofsky. 1985. *Between Men: English Literature and Male Homosocial Desire.* New York: Columbia University Press.

Selden, Daniel. 1992. *"Ceveat Lector:* Catullus and the Rhetoric of Performance." In Ralph Hexter and Daniel Selden, eds., *Innovations of Antiquity*, 461–512. New York: Routledge.

Skinner, Marilyn. 1989. *"Ut Decuit Cinaediorem:* Power, Gender and Urbanity in Catullus 10." *Helios* 16 (1989): 7–23.

Wiseman, T. P. 1985. *Catullus and His World: A Reappraisal.* Cambridge: Cambridge University Press.

Wray, David. 2001. *Catullus and the Poetics of Roman Manhood.* Cambridge: Cambridge University Press.

CHAPTER 2

A POET RESTORED
Contemporary Scholarship and the Teaching of Ovid

Barbara Weiden Boyd

PROLOGUE: EXILE AS LIFE AND AS METAPHOR

In an age when issues of identity, especially national identity, have become the focus of renewed interest for scholars in disciplines ranging from politics and philosophy to genetics and literary history, it is perhaps no surprise that the circumstances of exile and exiled writers in various historical periods have become freshly intriguing. Exile in its various forms was regularly used as an instrument of social and political control in the ancient world;[1] yet few ancient exiles have so fired the imagination as has Ovid, the cause of whose relegation in 8 C.E. to Tomis, on the shores of the Black (Euxine) Sea, remains in fact if not in theory an insoluble mystery.[2] In this essay, I consider some of the reasons why the work of Rome's most famous exiled poet has remained in virtual exile for so long, especially in our own modern American educational setting.[3] I want to emphasize that I use metaphors associated with exile throughout most of this discussion as simply (and powerfully) that—metaphors, and ones of modern origin. I do not think that exile was simply a metaphor for Ovid, however, although his exile poetry amply exploits its imaginative potential. It has in fact been recently proposed that the world of exile as depicted in Ovid's *Tristia* and *Epistulae ex Ponto* is actually an

21

elaborate literary hoax, no more literally historical than are the more than 250 mythological narratives incorporated into the *Metamorphoses*.[4] While I applaud the healthy skepticism that invites such theorizing, in this case I wish to redirect it, and explore here not the relative merits of fact and fiction per se but rather the ways in which Ovid's poetry invites us to speculate, as readers and as teachers, about the inextricable relationships between art and life, between thought and expression, between other and self, and between teaching and learning. My goal is to demonstrate a few of the ways in which Ovid's poetry should and can be restored to our students and to our understanding of Roman literary culture.

I. (AUTO)BIOGRAPHY AND POETRY

From childhood we are taught to make sense of the world around us and of ourselves by creating categories, and by locating the things and people we experience in these categories. The Ovid I met in college in the 1970s was already neatly categorized for me, as insincere, inferior, even degenerate in comparison to all of his predecessors in the great pageant of Latin writers; even the transparency of his versification was represented to me as a flaw. The near-perfection of Ovidian meters, characterized by the infrequency of elision or of any overpowering conflict between ictus and word accent, and complemented by Ovid's strong preference for disyllabic pentameter endings and discrete units of thought neatly contained by verse limits, has itself been a nearly fatal flaw for those seeking to categorize this poet.[5] Ovid has in effect been portrayed to many upon first encounter as a poetry machine, able to generate flawless hexameters and penta-meters at will, or even without any thought.[6] I did not really understand all of this when I was an undergraduate; I simply absorbed what I was taught, never questioning the categories that made a story, with beginning, middle, and end, out of the history of Latin literature. In that story, Ovid had the dubious distinction of bringing the "Golden Age of Latin Poetry" to a crass and abrupt end.[7]

During my time in graduate school, Ovid was again missing in action. I read a few selections from the *Metamorphoses* in a first-year reading course, the main goal of which was to get our reading up to speed; another student in the class, however, appalled by the predatory characterizations of Apollo in Book 1 and Tereus in Book 6, protested what she perceived to be Ovid's sadistic cruelty. The professor gracefully tolerated this student's inability to distinguish between the poet Ovid and his subject matter, and decided in short order to move on to Livy. (It is interesting to speculate what might have happened to our reading of Livy had the same student reacted in a similar way to Livy's narratives of the rape and suicide of Lucretia, and of the death of Servius Tullius, who was thrown down the palace steps by would-be assassins and then run over by his bloodthirsty daughter in the road, where he was left to die.) A few years later, I finally had the opportunity to read more than selections from Propertius and Tibullus in a graduate seminar on Roman elegy. I realize now, however, that even as I luxuriated in Propertian excess, there was something missing: twelve of the fourteen weeks in the elegy seminar were devoted to Propertius and Tibullus, the natural result of which was that the participants wrote their seminar reports and term papers on these two elegists. The *Amores* and *Ars amatoria,* meanwhile, were the objects of a quick frolic at the end of the term, and no one in the class seriously considered writing anything on Ovidian elegy. Thus, Ovid again played the role in which I had first experienced him when I was an undergraduate: the outsider, barely fit for genteel society, and a self-made literary degenerate, the ample survival of whose work was a clear indication of the randomness of fate. Had the tables been turned and had only the "good stuff" survived, it was clear (if only by implication), the Ovidian corpus would surely have evanesced, and the late-lamented *Amores* of Gallus would have endured to take its place. As if on cue, a new fragment of Gallus was shortly thereafter identified and published, to great fanfare, if not acclaim;[8] and even the second and third thoughts provoked by this fragment have not been able entirely to erase the primacy—of time, influence, and literary superiority—allotted to Gallus by the vagaries of political and literary history.[9]

In the early 1990s, I had been teaching at Bowdoin for more than ten years. Ovid had by then begun to undergo a profound reevaluation and rehabilitation in the scholarly ranks; one might compare what is happening now with the poets of the later first century C.E., such as Statius and Lucan, even Seneca (as tragedian), Silius Italicus, and Valerius Flaccus.[10] It is easy, if unnecessarily cynical, to explain this trend on one level as indicative of a group consensus among Latinists that the Augustan poets have been "done," and that this later generation welcomes the attention of dissertation writers everywhere who are eager to work on something with a relatively manageable bibliography. This explanation, however, while containing a kernel of accuracy insofar as earlier inattention is concerned, misses entirely the important point that the categories we impose on these and other writers and their texts—"Gold" vs. "Silver," first vs. last, innovator vs. imitator—are entirely external to the creative and historical worlds in which these poets lived and in which their poems were read. I do not mean to suggest that there is absolutely no difference in quality and appeal between, for example, Valerius Flaccus and Vergil, or between Silius and Ovid; but I urge readers to think carefully about the value of measuring quality and appeal (among other things) as somehow ahistorical and transcendent qualities of literary texts, and to recognize the far-reaching—if often unanticipated—consequences of these measurements.[11] As the last of those poets whom we conveniently categorize as "Augustan," Ovid has long been measured against Vergil, Horace, Tibullus, and Propertius, and judged, for some reason or other, to have failed. Reconsidered as a transitional figure, however—

as the first post-Augustan poet, in other words—Ovid sheds valuable light through his work not just on the underexplored later years of Augustus but on the ascendancy of Tiberius as well. The scholarly reassessment of Ovid in the 1980s had already begun to confront these alternative perspectives head-on and to suggest new avenues of approach; and as a teacher of undergraduates, I had the opportunity on an almost daily basis to advance this new approach, however implicitly. Indeed, it is primarily through the experience of reading Ovid with my own students, with fresh eyes free from the biases of established opinion, that I was able to begin to make sense of this poet on his own terms, and to recognize the way in which his recent reception is as much a reflection of contemporary concerns about identity and originality as it is about Ovid himself and what he wrote.

Around the same time, I began to work with the Advanced Placement (AP) Latin Test Development Committee coordinated by the Educational Testing Service (ETS); and, perhaps not entirely coincidentally, it was during my tenure on this committee that Ovid was introduced to the AP Latin curriculum, where he has since had remarkable success.[12] To some readers, this experience may seem to have little bearing on scholarly concerns, and virtually no connection at all to Ovid's scholarly reputation and his place in the college or postgraduate curriculum; indeed, most of my colleagues teaching at the college level have no particular interest in the status of AP Latin, other than as a quick (and not always accurate) means of assessing an entering college student's Latin ability. I want to suggest, however, that there is in fact a strong correlation between what is taught at the high school level in Latin classes and the way the students in those high school classes approach the study of Latin at the next stage of their education. Furthermore, the relationship between what is taught and how it is taught at the AP level has direct bearing on the attitudes about the study of Latin that students bring with them to college. My experience with the AP Latin program was, and continues to be, eye-opening, even as it serves as an important symbolic bridge between the introductory and advanced levels of Latin study, and between teaching and scholarship. Simply put, it offers a model for the relationship between pedagogy and scholarship suggested by the essays in this book and the panel presentations from which they developed.[13]

Ovid's introduction to and success in the AP Latin program are in fact closely linked to his newfound appeal among his scholarly readership. Furthermore, whereas it might originally have been said that scholarly fashion shaped the high school Latin curriculum, an argument can be made that the reverse plays a role as well: I now have students who have encountered Ovid already before entering college, and who carry with them from high school little if any negative bias regarding the poet. Thus, they want to read Ovid, and easily recognize the integral part he plays in the Latin literary tradition. They are reading the new scholarship on Ovid, and writing papers about him themselves. Ironically, their relative lack of historical awareness has only added to Ovid's allure: the richness of the *Metamorphoses* stands perfectly well on its own without the support of Vergil, and the humorous self-consciousness of the *Amores* nicely suits their own postmodern irony about themselves and their relationships with others. One of the most successful advanced Latin courses that I have taught in the last decade has been a seminar on the *Fasti*—a course that, practically speaking, would not have been possible until very recently, because of the lack of textbooks.[14] That poem's jarring and sometimes bizarre blend of myth, religion, astronomy, history, ritual, Callimachean aesthetics, and Augustan politics has an immediacy and an ostentatious cleverness about it that make it a remarkable resource for students of all things Roman. Thanks in no small part to his introduction into the high school curriculum—itself a result of scholarly energy and interest—Ovid has been restored, again and at last, to the Latin classroom; his exile is over.

II. THE POWER OF CATEGORIES

But my task here is not yet done. It has been my goal thus
far to sketch a kind of modern intellectual biography for Ovid and
his poetry, or—to use the exile metaphor—to trace his journey
from Tomis back to "Rome": the Latin classroom. I have also
tried to suggest how we, as scholars and teachers, have partici-
pated in the effort to make Ovid a citizen of Roman literature
again. It is time to turn to the practical side of my task: Now that
Ovid has been restored to us, how do we make the most of him
and his poetry for our students? And how do we avoid falling
into some of the old patterns of reception and criticism? To
put it another way, what exactly have we gained with Ovid's
restoration, and why is it worth having? Some of the ways in
which Ovid has been read—and, I think, misread—in the recent
past have had a profound effect on how we approach him. In the
process of countering these readings with a different approach,
furthermore, we can exploit misreading itself as an opportunity
for the "teachable moment." After all, we are, among other things,
teachers of reading; and as we work with our students through
a Latin text, we have the opportunity to show them not just what
to read but also how and why to read. My goal in my classes
is always, first and foremost, to teach my students how to ask
useful questions about their reading; and Ovid's poetry proves
to be fertile ground for this sort of work, rich as it is in humor,
ambivalence, and multiple meanings.

Humor, ambivalence, and multiple meanings are relative
newcomers in discussions of Ovid's poetry. Instead, the blurring
of style and substance as evaluative categories encouraged the
flourishing of a number of critical stereotypes about Ovid, well
summarized by Stephen Hinds in his 1987 article "Generalising
about Ovid."[15] Hinds identified three stereotypes dominating
twentieth-century Ovidian criticism: (1) the "shallow and over-
explicit" Ovid; (2) the "excessively literary" Ovid; and (3) the
"passive panegyrist" Ovid. I will use these categories in my

own discussion as well, although with some modification. In particular, the second category calls for a slightly different approach from that originally given it by Hinds, because much has changed in the study of Ovid in the eighteen years since Hinds wrote his essay, during which time a whole new generation of scholars, with new attitudes about classical studies in general and Ovid in particular, has matured and entered the profession. Furthermore, I want to add a fourth category, the importance of which has achieved a certain independent status—while remaining in some ways a subset of Ovid's alleged shallowness and over-explicitness—only since Hinds' essay appeared: viz., Ovid's apparent self-indulgence in a certain violent aestheticism in his literary treatment of sexual relations, reflecting as it does the discourses of power and gender that informed the Roman literary imagination. Few scholarly readers nowadays would be inclined to object to Ovid's literariness per se, even in its sometimes extreme manifestations. The intertextuality of ancient literature, and especially of Latin poetry, has come to dominate discussions not only of Ovid but of virtually every major Latin text, and the brilliance of Ovidian practice in this area is on display in almost all of the studies that appear in the list of references appended to this essay. But the relationship between Ovid's evident control over his raw material and his apparent lack, even deconstruction, of raw emotion remains, to some extent, at least, a locus of readerly disease—the gap between the poet and his work remains difficult for many readers to negotiate, if only because the surface is so perfect. The increasing attention given to Ovid's poetry in recent feminist scholarship has also heightened readers' awareness of the role played by sexual politics in destabilizing the relationship between the poet and his readers. I want, therefore, to consider a few selections from our poet in some detail, and to suggest that Ovid wants us to be curious not only about the perfect surface of his poetry and what lies beneath, but also about the relationship between the two—about not only the what and the how, but also the why. To

borrow a metaphor from the world of hypertext, Ovid is perhaps
the most reader-oriented and interactive of the Latin poets; as
readers, we have both the opportunity and the responsibility to
engage him on his own terms.

III. The Meandering Reader

It is not my intention to tell you what the passages I have
chosen to look at "mean," or how to interpret them; rather, my
goal is to provide a few examples of the sort of question-asking
strategies that can be very productive with Ovid. I have intentionally chosen passages or excerpts that have invited negative
criticism from the perspective of one or more of the categories
described above, and I suggest that the strong reaction we
have to them, positive or negative or, more interestingly, both, is
exactly what Ovid intended. I also plan to consider the Ovidian
corpus as a whole, rather than restricting myself to already
familiar texts, in hopes of imparting to you my own convic-
tion that the more widely in the Ovidian corpus we read, the
better equipped we are to contextualize individual passages
and poems.

First I want to turn to the very first Ovidian poem I read as
an undergraduate: *Amores* 1.9. This choice does not, on its face,
suit my own avowed desire to introduce my readers to some of
Ovid's less familiar works; in fact, this elegy is often used—as
it was in my case—to represent Ovid *pars pro toto*. In looking
at it here, however, I go out of my way to "defamiliarize" it, by
putting it back into its literary and historical contexts. It also
deserves our immediate attention because it so perfectly typifies
Hinds' "shallow and over-explicit" category, so long at the heart
of modern assent to Ovid's continuing exile; and, as will become
evident, it simultaneously allows us to consider how violence
informs Ovid's imagined erotic world. Let us begin with the
opening couplet:

Militat omnis amans, et habet sua castra Cupido;
Attice, crede mihi, militat omnis amans.

Every lover is a soldier, and Cupid has his own camp;
Atticus, believe me, every lover is a soldier.[16]

From the very first line, this poem announces its contrary nature,
with the pairing of love and war, a pairing as old as ancient
literature itself. We find clearly formulated, both in Homer and
in Empedocles and the other pre-Socratic philosophers, the idea
that love and war are two cosmic opposites. The plot of the *Iliad*
reenacts, in the competition between Agamemnon and Achilles
for Briseis, the earlier competition between Paris and Menelaus
for Helen; Homeric lovers are warriors, and vice versa. In Empedocles' vision of the cosmic order, creation is the result of unceasing
alteration between Love and Strife; expressed in hexameter verse,
Empedocles' cosmic philosophy asserts the fundamental inseparability of these complementary elements, whose interaction is
what causes all things to come into existence and time to begin.[17]
The pairing of love and war is central to the mythic cosmogony
of Book 1 of Lucretius' *De rerum natura,* depicting the seduction of Mars by Venus (1.29–40); and the similar seduction of
Vulcan by Venus at *Aeneid* 8.370–406, as the goddess convinces
the god to make new weapons for her son, likewise elevates
the interrelationship of love and war to the cosmic scale. Both
Lucretius and Vergil look back to Homer for an epic paradigm,
and find it in the tale told by Demodocus at the court of the
Phaeacians in *Odyssey* 8: the story recounted there, of Ares and
Aphrodite's betrayal of Hephaestus, encapsulates the inextricable
association of love and strife even as it offers comic relief to an
audience emotionally wearied by the tales of war that preceded
it. Ovid's "shallow" analogy thus plumbs the rich depths of
literary tradition.

In the course of the poem, Ovid invites his reader to make
at least some of these associations explicit, as he catalogues other

lovers besides himself who were warriors, and vice versa, and
their shared stratagems (*Am.* 1.9.21–40):

saepe soporatos invadere profuit hostes
    caedere et armata vulgus inerme manu.
sic fera Threicii ceciderunt agmina Rhesi,
    et dominum capti deseruistis equi.
nempe maritorum somnis utuntur amantes   25
    et sua sopitis hostibus arma movent.
custodum transire manus vigilumque catervas
    militis et miseri semper amantis opus.
Mars dubius, nec certa Venus: victique resurgunt,
    quosque neges umquam posse iacere, cadunt.   30
ergo desidiam quicumque vocabat amorem,
    desinat: ingenii est experientis Amor.
ardet in abducta Briseide magnus Achilles
    (dum licet, Argeas frangite, Troes, opes);
Hector ab Andromaches complexibus ibat ad arma,   35
    et galeam capiti quae daret, uxor erat.
summa ducum, Atrides visa Priameide fertur
    Maenadis effusis obstipuisse comis.
Mars quoque deprensus fabrilia vincula sensit:
    notior in caelo fabula nulla fuit.   40

It has often been advantageous to attack enemy troops while they slept,
    and to slaughter the unarmed crowd with weapons at the ready.
Thus the fierce battle lines of Thracian Rhesus fell,
    And thus, captured horses, did you desert your master.
Lovers, to be sure, take advantage of husbands' sleep
    And raise their own weapons while the enemy slumbers.
To get through bands of guards and troops of watchmen
    Is always the task of the soldier—and of the unfortunate lover.
Mars is unpredictable, and Venus, unreliable: the defeated rise again,
    And those who you would say could never lie low, do indeed fall.
Whoever called love "laziness," therefore,
    Should stop: Love has an industrious nature.

Great Achilles burns for stolen Briseis
    (while you can, Trojans, break the Argive troops);
Hector went from Andromache's embrace straight to war,
    And the one to put the helmet on his head was his wife.
Having caught sight of Priam's daughter, Agamemnon, greatest
    of leaders, is said to have been dumbstruck by the Maenad's
    flowing hair.
Mars, too, caught *in flagrante delicto,* felt the artisan's chains:
    No tale was more famous in heaven.

From the night raid on Rhesus' camp (21–24) to Achilles' love for Briseis, Hector's for Andromache, and Agamemnon's for Cassandra (33–38), Ovid's frame of reference is the *Iliad;* and his allusion to the story of Venus and Mars in 39–40, preceded by the pairing of their names in a couplet rich in sexual double entendre (29–30),[18] explicitly evokes the story told at *Odyssey* 8.266–369. In other words, Ovid's frame of reference is not just generically mythological but specifically literary, specifically epic, and specifically Homeric. He thus neatly challenges the very nature of the poetry he is writing—if you believe that love and war are just like each other, then you will also believe that Ovid is just like Homer, that elegy is just like epic, and that the *Amores* are just like the *Iliad* and *Odyssey.*

The repetition of *militat omnis amans* in the two halves of the first couplet drives the oxymoron home, even as it models the repetitiousness of the love-and-war twosome throughout their long literary life together. The address to his friend Atticus, along with the emphatic words *crede mihi,* adds to our awareness of the self-consciousness of Ovid's artifice even as it problematizes the impression of sincerity it evokes: Is Ovid's opening assertion actually true, in the real, as opposed to the literary, world? In other words, is it actually possible to write elegies about love without resorting to poetic clichés, without being "excessively literary"? Are love and love poetry inextricably linked, or mutually exclusive?

Ovid's clearly self-conscious literary excess (itself so brilliantly controlled) thus invites a subversive reading, one that not only exposes the analogy's logical flaws but also mirrors those of the world around it. Catullus (among others) used poetry to polarize the worlds in which love and war prevail; the shockingly non-Sapphic conclusion to his evocation of Sappho's vividly physical experience of love in c. 51 juxtaposes the spheres of *otium* and *negotium* (9–16):[19]

> lingua sed torpet, tenuis sub artus
> flamma demanat, sonitu suopte
> tintinant aures, gemina teguntur
>   lumina nocte.
>
> otium, Catulle, tibi molestum est:
> otio exsultas nimiumque gestis:
> otium et reges prius et beatas
>   perdidit urbes.

> But my tongue is numb, and a slender flame
> Flows down into my limbs; my ears ring
> With their own sound, and my eyes are cloaked
>   With twin night.
>
> Leisure, Catullus, is troublesome to you:
> In leisure you take pleasure, and you desire it too much.
> Leisure in former times destroyed both kings
>   And fortunate cities.

In *Amores* 1.9, Ovid can be seen to blend the two worlds of *otium* and *negotium,* or even to turn them on their heads, through a succinct rejection of the Catullan world-view based on a clever redefinition of the *vita desidiosa* ("life of leisure"):

> ergo desidiam quicumque vocabat amorem,
>   desinat: ingenii est experientis Amor (31–32).

Whoever called love "laziness," therefore,
Should stop: Love has an industrious nature.

While willfully trivializing war, the macho pursuit par excellence
of Roman men, Ovid also makes the emotional experiences of
the lover seem deceptive and violent (see especially 17–28);
while "epicizing" love (*qui nolet fieri desidiosus, amet,* "he who
does not wish to become a sluggard should love," 46), he is also
asserting the elegiac affinities of epic. The elaborate equation
established in this elegy between love and war also hints at a
theme that Ovid develops explicitly elsewhere in the *Amores:* the
potential use of epic models to legitimize the aggressive violence
of an elegiac lover in pursuit of erotic conquest and domination.[20] And then, because he is Ovid, he stops, implicitly inviting
us to challenge the implications of his reasoned comparison of
love and war even as he refrains from delineating the likely consequences of moving from battlefield to bed[21] (or vice versa, for
that matter). To fix a monolithic interpretation here—to decide
whether or not this poem is shallow—is not really the point, it
seems to me; the essential thing, and the one that gives this
poem its distinctively Ovidian insouciance, is our recognition of
and participation in the questioning process that Ovid invites with
his words *crede mihi.* The rest of the poem depends on those
two little words, after all, and the tone we give to them.[22]

Let me offer another example of how Ovid opens up his
poetry to simultaneous varied readings. The following example
has also been chosen to demonstrate that what I have just suggested about the participatory nature of Ovidian verse is a repeated
and indeed quite instructive compositional technique in our poet.
The second passage I look at is from Ovid's *Fasti;* I have chosen
something from this poem in part so that I can direct my readers'
attention to the fact that much of the most exciting scholarship
published in recent years is on this poem, and so that I can
encourage the inclusion of the *Fasti* in my readers' own study of
Ovid's work.[23] *Fasti* 2 is devoted to the various holidays, religious

rituals, and other important events in the civil calendar for the month of February. One of these days, the Nones, is the anniversary of Augustus' receipt, in 2 B.C.E., of the title *pater patriae,* bestowed upon him by the Senate at the dedication of the forum of Augustus. Ovid draws our attention to the importance of this occasion, and the concomitant weightiness of his poetic task, with an introductory eight lines (four couplets) in which, as in *Amores* 1.9, he asserts the relationship of subject matter and poetic genre:

Nunc mihi mille sonos quoque est memoratus Achilles
    vellem, Maeonide, pectus inesse tuum,   120
dum canimus sacras alterno carmine Nonas.
    maximus hic fastis accumulatur honos.
deficit ingenium, maioraque viribus urgent:
    haec mihi praecipuo est ore canenda dies.
quid volui demens elegis imponere tantum   125
    ponderis? heroi res erat ista pedis.

Now I wish I had a thousand sounding voices, O Maeonian poet, and that
    The inspired power with which you memorialized Achilles were in me.
While I with my elegiac couplets sing of the sacred Nones,
    Supreme honor is heaped up on the calendar.
Inspiration is wanting, and these themes demand strength greater than mine:
    I must sing of this day with exceptional poetic effort.
Why, fool that I am, did I wish to burden my elegies with
    So great a weight? Epic meter would have suited this subject.

Whereas in the earlier poem Ovid played upon the alleged inseparability of epic war and elegiac love, here the poet suggests an extreme split between the two—he apologizes for using elegiac meter for a theme that deserves hexameter (126). Note how Achilles and Homer are mentioned by name in the first couplet here, and so bring epic themes, especially those of the *Iliad*, powerfully into our frame of reference. Much as in *Amores* 1.9, they not only serve to draw our attention to the relationship of subject matter and style but also urge us to think about the choices our poet makes. The very inclusion of Achilles and Homer in an elegiac poem is, after all, a challenge to generic expectations—and to emphasize that the impossible has indeed been made possible, Ovid even addresses Homer directly, as if the two poets were not separated by the chasms of culture, time, theme, and genre.[24]

After eight lines asserting an inability to rise to the occasion, Ovid does just that, as his opening appeal to Homer gives way to an address to Augustus (127–32):

> sancte pater patriae, tibi plebs, tibi curia nomen
>   hoc dedit, hoc dedimus nos tibi nomen, eques.
> res tamen ante dedit: sero quoque vera tulisti
>   nomina, iam pridem tu pater orbis eras.
> hoc tu per terras, quod in aethere Iuppiter alto,
>   nomen habes: hominum tu pater, ille deum.

> Blessed father of our country, to you the plebeians, to you the Senate
>   Have given this name; we equestrians too give this name to you.
> History, however, gave it to you earlier; in fact, only late in the
> day have you acquired
>   Your true name—you have actually been father of the world
>   for some time now.
> On earth you have the name which Jupiter holds
>   In high heaven: you are the father of men, and he, of gods.

The words *pater* and *nomen* each appear more than once in the first two couplets (*pater* twice, echoed for a third time in the single appearance of *patria; nomen* three times); each is repeated once more in the third couplet (131–32) as well. The effect of these repetitions, as with that of *militat omnis amans* in the opening couplet of *Amores* 1.9, is to underline the parallels alleged in the passage: Augustus deserves to be called *pater patriae,* for he has long since been acclaimed as *pater orbis;* and the word *pater* is as apt a *nomen* for him on this earth, this *orbis,* as it is when used to describe Jupiter in heaven.

After the bold assertion of equivalence between man and god in 132 (*hominum tu pater, ille deum*), Ovid redirects his attention (and ours) again in the next couplet and suggests yet another parallel, replacing Jupiter with Romulus as Augustus' *comparandus.* Ovid thus implies (but notice, it is only implicit) that to compare Augustus with Jupiter may be just slightly too daring after all; so now Jupiter is replaced with Romulus—indeed, Romulus now becomes the object of Ovid's direct address (133–44):

> Romule, concedes: facit hic tua magna tuendo
>   moenia, tu dederas transilienda Remo.
> te Tatius parvique Cures Caeninaque sensit,   135
>   hoc duce Romanum est solis utrumque latus;
> tu breve nescioquid victae telluris habebas,
>   quodcumque est alto sub Iove, Caesar habet.
> tu rapis, hic castas duce se iubet esse maritas;
>   tu recipis luco, reppulit ille nefas;   140
> vis tibi grata fuit, florent sub Caesare leges;
>   tu domini nomen, principis ille tenet;
> te Remus incusat, veniam dedit hostibus ille;
>   caelestem fecit te pater, ille patrem.

> You must admit it, Romulus: by protecting your walls he makes them
>   Great, while you allowed them to be jumped over by Remus.
> Tatius and little Cures and Caenina felt your might,
>   While under this leader each side of the sun is Roman;
> You possessed a little bit of conquered territory,
>   While Augustus Caesar possesses whatever lies beneath lofty
>   Jupiter.
> You commit rape; he orders married women to be chaste while he rules;
>   You welcome criminals into the asylum, while he has driven
>   out the unspeakable.

Force gave you pleasure, while laws flourish under Augustus Caesar;
You have the title of master, while he has the title of prince.
Remus lays the blame on you, while this leader pardoned his enemies;
Your father Mars made you a god, Romulus, while this man
has deified his father Julius Caesar.

The verb *concedes* in 133, like *crede mihi* in *Am.* 1.9.2, immediately invites both Ovid's nominal addressee and his modern readers to consider whether this comparison is indeed appropriate. Ovid then devotes the remainder of this passage to an explicit and direct comparison of the relative merits of Augustus and Romulus—"Augustus protects the very walls that you, Romulus, allowed Remus to jump over; Augustus has conquered the world, while you, Romulus, reached barely the Roman suburbs in your quest for world domination; Augustus is the protector of chaste women, while you, Romulus, were their rapist; Augustus averts all that is *nefas,* while you, Romulus, welcomed it into the *asylum* of early Rome; Augustus rules with law, while you, Romulus, used violence; Augustus shows mercy where you, Romulus, showed none." The culmination of this catalogue appears in the last line I have quoted, where Ovid reminds us once again of the role of the word *pater* in this passage even as he plays with its multiple associations—now the fathers of Romulus and of Augustus are recalled, Mars and Julius Caesar respectively, and we discover that Augustus really has more in common with the divine Mars than with Mars' son. The implied parallel suggested here between Augustus and a god—a parallel from which Ovid had veered away after first suggesting a similarity between Augustus and Jupiter in 131–32—thus proves to be appropriate after all, it seems, and the manifest destiny of Augustan Rome is guaranteed by the leader's divine dispensation.

Readers will not be surprised to learn that the interpretation of this passage is wildly controversial. It has received many different treatments in recent years, and while almost everyone agrees that Ovid's wit is in abundant supply here, the reasons for and the results of its display are far less easily agreed upon.[25] Are we to believe that Ovid intends to compliment Augustus by comparing him to Romulus, or to suggest a sly insult? After all, Octavian is reported to have considered taking the name "Romulus" as honorific before settling on "Augustus" instead;[26] if our sources on this are at all reliable, Octavian himself would appear to have held Rome's first founder in great esteem. At the same time, the portrayal of Romulus in Livy's canonical account of Rome's origins suggests that his character and motivations were the subject of heated debate in first-century B.C.E. Rome.[27] A slightly different approach would suggest that the point of the comparison is really not to do offense to the memory of Romulus at all, but rather to show how even his accomplishments are as nothing when compared to those of his great successor. When the episode is seen from this perspective, no insult or other form of detriment to Romulus would seem to be intended by Ovid; praise is the singular goal of the poet, even spontaneous panegyric, and Romulus serves as the perfect foil for Augustus precisely because of his own defining role in Roman history.[28] This passage is, in fact, a wonderful candidate for inclusion in the briefs of those who allege the accuracy of a "passive panegyrist" characterization of Ovid.

When I read Book 2 of the *Fasti* with my undergraduate students, I find that this passage provides an ideally "teachable moment" in our ongoing discussion of Ovidian narrative techniques. It also quite obviously gets at a question of fundamental importance for our understanding of Ovid's engagement of the Augustan regime. I would like to suggest here just a few of the opportunities for discussion and analysis provoked by this passage. First, of course, is the question of context: the passage is not, after all, a discrete elegy, but an integral part of the variably textured fabric of *Fasti* 2. A first attempt at disentangling the complexity of this episode, therefore, would necessarily entail a discussion of Book 2 in its entirety. But other opportunities present themselves as well: for example, we might undertake an examination of all of the episodes in the *Fasti* that involve Romulus. Such an examination would quickly reveal that Ovid's treatment of Romulus is something of a moving target, characterized as he is throughout the poem by both *pietas* and fratricide—in some cases, in the same episode.[29] And we could move outside the boundaries of the *Fasti* as well: to take but two prominent examples, we might look at the depiction of Romulus that sets the patriotic (or "patriotic") agenda for the *Ars amatoria*, as Ovid uses the rape of the Sabine women to give the young men of Rome a politically correct rationale for seeking out prospective sexual partners at the theater (*AA* 1.89–134), or at the apotheosis of Romulus with which *Metamorphoses* 14 culminates (778–828).[30] In undertaking such comparisons, my goal as teacher is not to assert the rightness or wrongness of a particular reading or readings—although of course I want my students to know and be able to articulate for themselves which arguments for a particular point of view are strong, and which are less so. Most important to me is that my students come away from discussions such as this with at least a tiny shred of doubt about whether they really have reached a single, stable interpretation of the passage(s) under consideration—as indeed Augustus himself must have felt after he had finished making his way through Ovid's brilliant combination of self-effacing *recusatio* and verbal pyrotechnics. I would also like my students to begin to realize that, as with *Amores* 1.9, there is a kind of deconstruction of cultural conventions going on in the episode from *Fasti* 2 cited above, as the character of Romulus raises questions about the character of Augustus, and vice versa. Love and war, Romulus and Augustus—how fundamental is their interdependence, and does it mean the same thing to modern readers as it once did to Ovid's Roman audience?

I conclude with a slightly different sort of example, again selected from among the many passages that have attracted critical comment and discussion.[31] This excerpt is from the story of Daedalus, which appears in Book 8 of the *Metamorphoses*.[32] The passage I wish to focus on is generally considered transitional, as it serves to separate the preceding major narrative of Scylla from the next big story, the flight of Daedalus and Icarus. The distinction between "major" and "minor" episodes, between transitions and the dominant plot, however, is a continually tested boundary in the *Metamorphoses,* and one to which Ovid continually, and ostentatiously, draws his readers' attention. As I repeatedly suggest to my students, if Ovid chose to include this episode in his narrative, he must have felt that it served some purpose and had some narrative appeal; it would be foolhardy blithely to assume that he included it simply because he felt that it was "traditional" or "necessary." Ovid's mastery of his material is such (as, in fact, this very scene shows), and his interest in his readers is so profound, that they would do well not to dismiss this as any less integral to the *Metamorphoses* than are the more extended scenes that surround it. Rather, the transitions found throughout the *Metamorphoses* provide a fascinating opportunity to see how Ovid thinks about his material and engages his readers.[33]

    I quote the passage under consideration here in full (*Met.* 8.152–82):

Vota Iovi Minos taurorum corpora centum
solvit, ut egressus ratibus Curetida terram
contigit, et spoliis decorata est regia fixis.
creverat opprobrium generis foedumque patebat   155
matris adulterium monstri novitate biformis;
destinat hunc Minos thalami removere pudorem
multiplicique domo caecisque includere tectis.
Daedalus ingenio fabrae celeberrimus artis
ponit opus turbatque notas et lumina flexa   160
ducit in errorem variarum ambage viarum.
non secus ac liquidis Phrygius Maeandros in undis
ludit et ambiguo lapsu refluitque fluitque
occurrensque sibi venturas aspicit undas
et nunc ad fontes, nunc ad mare versus apertum   165
incertas exercet aquas, ita Daedalus implet

innumeras errore vias vixque ipse reverti
ad limen potuit; tanta est fallacia tecti.

quo postquam geminam tauri iuvenisque figuram
clausit et Actaeo bis pastum sanguine monstrum   170
tertia sors annis domuit repetita novenis,
utque ope virginea nullis iterata priorum
ianua difficilis filo est inventa relecto,
protinus Aegides rapta Minoide Dian
vela dedit comitemque suam crudelis in illo   175
litore destituit. desertae et multa querenti
amplexus et opem Liber tulit, utque perenni
sidere clara foret, sumptam de fronte coronam
immisit caelo; tenues volat illa per auras
dumque volat gemmae nitidos vertuntur in ignes   180
consistuntque loco, specie remanente coronae,
qui medius Nixique genu est Anguemque tenentis.

Minos paid off his vow to Jupiter, 100 bodies of bulls, when he
disembarked from his ship and touched the Cretan land; the
palace was decorated with spoils affixed. The family's shame had
grown, and the mother's despicable adultery was revealed by the
novel strangeness of the biform creature; Minos determines to
remove this disgrace of his bedroom and to shut it up in the blind
alleys of a many-chambered dwelling.

Most renowned for his talent in the builder's craft, Daedalus
sets up the project, confusing everything recognizable, and with
the twisted duplicity of various paths leads the eyes astray. In the
same way, the Phrygian Meander plays in the liquid waters, and
with bi-directional gliding flows back and flows again, and as it
looks at the waters approaching runs into itself; now it urges on the
uncertain streams to their source, now again to the open sea. Just
so does Daedalus fill the countless paths with confusion; indeed, he
himself was scarcely able to return to the threshold, so great is the
deceptiveness of the edifice.

After he shut the double form of bull and youth within, the
third lottery, demanded every nine years, tamed the beast, fed twice

before on Attic blood; when thanks to a girl's help the difficult door, revisited by no one of earlier generations, was found with thread retraced, straightaway Theseus son of Aegeus set sail for Dia, having taken Ariadne, the daughter of Minos, with him, and then cruelly abandoned his companion on that shore. Bacchus brought both help and embraces to her, deserted as she was and much lamenting, and so that she might be renowned with an enduring star, he set the wreath taken from her forehead in the sky. That constellation flies through the slender breezes, and as it flies, the gems in the crown are transformed into shining fires. Her wreaths, their appearance remaining, now stay in one place, between the one on his knees, Engonasin, and the one holding Anguis.

Consider first of all the simile comparing the labyrinth to the river Meander (8.159–68). Like other extended similes, this one, describing the movement of a river through territory far distant from the Cretan labyrinth, is used by Ovid to suggest the presence of stories within stories.[34] In this case, the "story" told by the simile parallels the construction of the *Metamorphoses* itself, an artfully confusing sequence of interlocking stories, the narrative thread of which is soon lost. Inside this narrative labyrinth, however, there is in fact linear movement from point A to point B, and so on; as readers, we simply need to persevere, and let the meandering narrative take its time. It can hardly be coincidence that this description appears in the central book of the *Metamorphoses,* embedded as deeply within the poem as it can be. Ovid's narratorial comment on the relationship of Daedalus and his creation, *tanta est fallacia tecti,* could just as easily be applied to our relationship with the poem as we enter it through reading.[35]

Ovid then proceeds in fourteen lines to summarize what some readers might consider "the" story of the labyrinth, namely the story of Theseus and Ariadne, best known to Ovid's readers from Catullus c. 64 and alluded to prominently—and, not coincidentally, also at the center of the poem—by Vergil in his description of the doors on the temple of Apollo at Cumae, built by Daedalus himself (*Aen.* 6.14–33). Ovid's narrative races us through this complex story in little more than ten hexameters, with each line summarizing at least one major episode in the story. In 169, the Minotaur is introduced; in 170, the creature is shut in the labyrinth and then conquers two groups of youths sent as Athenian tribute; in 171, the tables are turned when the third group reaches Crete. In 172, we learn of Ariadne's desire to help; in 173, of the thread that guides Theseus; and in 174, of Theseus' subsequent carrying off of Ariadne. In 175, Theseus' cruelty comes to the fore, and in 176, his abandonment of her and her despair. In 177, Bacchus appears on the scene—and suddenly the narrative race comes to a halt as Ovid draws the line to a close with the word *perenni.* In 177, Ariadne's crown is transformed into a heavenly constellation, and remains fixed in the sky on permanent and timeless display. Likewise, the story ends—and just as the reader moves on, so does Daedalus, into the story of his fateful flight.

The "excessively literary" relationship of this episode to the poetry of Catullus and Vergil is perhaps one explanation for the general disregard of this passage—Ovid's haste, some might say, is a sign that he himself is eager to be finished with this story, and not to linger over something that has been done (and, the critical implication is, done better) before. But I want to close with the suggestion that if we treat this as a transitional passage and nothing more, we do so at our peril. Ovid uses this very episode, I believe, to comment on the nature of the relationship between a poet and his audience, to demonstrate his own mastery of his material, to alert us to the fact that he is not like any other poet we have ever read before, and to invite us to join him in the endlessly alluring game of entering into and escaping from the literary labyrinth of the *Metamorphoses.* Meanwhile, this episode demonstrates that Ovid's poem is something more than a chaotic collection of neatly narrated myths; it invites Ovid's readers to think about not only what they read but how they do so, and about the choices that constantly face both

storytellers and their audiences—to tell or not to tell, to detail
or to summarize, to listen or not. As teachers, we face these difficult choices every day. Reading
Ovid offers not an answer or a solution, but a thread with which
to negotiate our way through such choices. When we take hold
of the thread, we become participants in the restoration of Ovid
to the world of Roman poetry. I therefore invite new readers of
Ovid who come to him with at least some distance from those
biases so neatly captured by Hinds and tested against the above
excerpts to welcome Ovid wholeheartedly back into their classrooms—and to discover one more way to sustain the energy of
the discipline we share.

NOTES

1. On the forms of exile in the ancient world, see *OCD*[3], ss.vv.
ostracism (MacDowell, 1083); *exile, Roman* (Nicholas, 580); and *relegation* (Nicholas, 1297–98). See also Claassen 1999 for an overview
of literary treatments.

2. See Thibault 1964 for a comprehensive (but inconclusive)
assemblage of theories. Most modern scholars agree that Ovid himself
leads his readers to the likely assumption that the *Ars amatoria* was
the proximate cause for his relegation, although he is never really
explicit about this; see White 2002 for a clear exposition of the facts
(and non-facts) surrounding Ovid's life and career.

3. Although it is outside the limits of this essay, it is worth noting
that in many respects, the twentieth-century reception of Ovid is
anomalous, given his central place in the schoolroom and his resulting
powerful influence upon modes of literary, artistic, and ethical expression for much of the second millennium C.E. in the West.

4. Fitton Brown 1985. His hypothesis has met with much discussion, but not general acceptance.

5. Regarding elision, Otis offers the following comparison: "the
proportion of elisions to the total of lines in the whole *Aeneid* and

Metamorphoses is 15.6% for Ovid and 50.3% for Virgil" (1970, 75). For a sound discussion of all aspects of Ovidian versification, see Kenney 2002. Platnauer 1951 is an accessible reference for readers interested in the historical development of Latin elegiac verse.

6. For a less jaundiced view of Ovid's "instinctive" versification, see Goold 1965, 24, and cf. Boyd 1997, 29–30.

7. For a fuller exploration of the "progressive fallacy" vis-à-vis Ovid and its consequences, see my introductory chapter in Boyd 1997, especially 5–8; for the gold-and-silver-ages metaphor (the "biometallic fallacy"), see Farrell 2001, chap. 4.

8. See Anderson, Parsons, and Nisbet 1979.

9. For a helpful summary of the scholarly disappointment met by the fragment and a defense of its authenticity and style, see Fairweather 1984.

10. E.g., Hardie 1993 and Hershkowitz 1998.

11. See n. 7, above.

12. This committee is composed of an equal number of secondary- and college-level Latin teachers, plus the chief reader for the Latin tests (a college-level Latinist who coordinates and manages the grading of the exams each year) and two liaisons from ETS, whose job it is to guide the committee members in every aspect of the examinations' consistency, difficulty, coverage, and fairness. I served on this committee for a total of seven years: 1989–94 and 1995–97.

13. When I joined the Test Development Committee, the annual number of test takers on the Vergil Exam, then close to 2,000, was showing a steady but slow increase; meanwhile, the number of test takers on the Catullus-Horace Exam was stagnating at just below 800. As anyone whose child has recently paid to take an AP exam knows, ETS is a business: in 2003–2004, the cost to take a single AP examination was $82. Particularly in tight economic times, there can be a general worry in the air that the exams with smaller audiences may be vulnerable to budget cuts. Such was the case with the Catullus-Horace Exam; its lack of growth even as the Vergil Exam was reaching more students every year was a nagging concern. The committee decided that something had to be done to reach out to the Latin constituency, and to see how the numbers of Catullus-Horace test takers could be

expanded. We therefore circulated a few possible options, one of which was to replace the Catullus-Horace Exam with an Ovid or Catullus-Ovid test. Coincidentally, two of the members of the Test Development Committee were vocal Ovid enthusiasts, and were sure that an Ovid syllabus could be both appealing and successful. But the reaction to this idea was far from well received; in fact, the committee received several letters from long-time AP Latin teachers who vehemently protested the very thought of an AP Ovid exam. The reactions, biases, and questions that filled those letters amply demonstrated that the scholarly revival of Ovid had not—at least not yet—found a way to appeal to the audience of secondary-level Latin teachers. How could the Test Development Committee even think of replacing the golden Latin of sublime Horace with the inferior, second-rate, irreverent, even degenerate Ovid? The committee's critics were inadvertent descendants of Augustus: if the *princeps* thought that Ovid deserved his *relegatio,* their reasoning ran, so should we moderns.

The legacy of the committee's desire to institute change and growth in the AP Latin program and of the original chilly response to that idea survives in today's AP Latin examinations: the Latin Literature Exam, first given in 1999 as the replacement for the Catullus-Horace Exam, tests students on a pair of authors (the syllabus provides for three possible pairings). To accommodate the need for a statistically consistent means to measure performance on all three versions, Catullus serves as the "control" on each version of the exam; and in the case of the three optional authors, Horace, Cicero, and Ovid, selections are chosen for the syllabus that will, whenever possible, allow both AP students and their teachers to make meaningful connections between the two writers. The Ovid option in particular appears to have reached a new group of teachers and students; and even the challenge presented by the *Amores,* that would-be nail in the coffin of elegy, has not stopped this version of the AP Latin Literature Exam from being taught. In 2003, more than 59 percent of those taking the AP Latin Literature Exam chose the Catullus-Ovid option. That year, the total number of students taking the AP Vergil Exam was 3,788; the total number of those taking the Latin Literature Exam was 2,629 (distributed as Catullus-Cicero, 11.2 percent; Catullus-Horace, 29.4 percent; and Catullus-Ovid, 59.4 percent).

14. In addition to Fantham 1998, see the useful Bryn Mawr commentaries on Book 2 by Miller (1985) and on Book 5 by Nagle (1996).

15. Hinds 1987.

16. All translations are my own.

17. The importance of Empedoclean cosmogony in the intellectual and literary history of the ancient world has only recently begun to earn the recognition it deserves. For a valuable assessment, see Sedley 1998.

18. See McKeown 1989.

19. See Knox 1984.

20. The locus classicus for erotic violence in Ovid is *Am.* 1.7, in which the poet describes his own assault on Corinna. For a helpful introduction to Ovid's deployment of *militia amoris* throughout the *Amores,* see Cahoon 1988; and cf. Greene 1998, esp. chap. 4, on *Am.* 1.7 in particular. More generally on the stylistic play between artistic control and *furor* in the poem, see Boyd 1997, 122–30.

21. The terminology is Cahoon's (1988).

22. For further discussion of this elegy, see Boyd 1997, 160–63.

23. See, e.g., Newlands 1995; Herbert-Brown 1994 and 2002; Barchiesi 1997; and Boyd 2000 and 2003. Fantham (1995) provides a useful overview, and is herself the author of several important articles on the *Fasti:* honoris causa I note 1985 and 1992.

24. The mention of Homer is itself embedded in an allusion to one of Homer's most famously self-conscious moments, as he asks the Muses for help when he embarks upon the Catalogue of Ships (*Il.* 2.484–93).

25. For an introduction to the issues at stake here, see Barchiesi 1997, 101–12 (= 1994, 112–23); Newlands 1995, 188–90; and Herbert-Brown 1994, chap. 2. All of these scholars in turn offer guidance to additional bibliography on the passage.

26. So Dio Cassius 53.16; according to Suetonius, *Augustus* 7, the Senate was responsible for the suggestion that the name "Romulus" be bestowed as an honorific.

27. See Ogilvie 1965 on Livy 1.3.10–1.16.

28. Indeed, as one of the anonymous readers for this essay has suggested, it might even be possible to read in these lines a subtle critique of Augustus' audacity in deifying Julius Caesar. While this reading had

not occurred to me, Ovid's playful alternation in this passage between praise and blame, and between Romulus and Augustus, certainly invites such a variant reading.

29. Other major episodes involving Romulus in the *Fasti* include 4.807–62 and 5.451–80. For a detailed analysis of the last of these, see Boyd 2000, 86–93.

30. On the rape of the Sabines in *AA* 1, see Watson 2002, 152–54; on the apotheosis of Romulus in *Met.* 14, see Tissol 2002, 326–32. Both provide discussion and bibliography.

31. See, e.g., Hollis 1970 and Crabbe 1981.

32. Teachers and students interested in looking at how Ovid can use the same story for different purposes in very different poems may wish to compare the Daedalus and Icarus narrative in *AA* 2.21–96.

33. For an enlightening discussion of how Ovid exploits the ends of books, see Holzberg 1998.

34. On Ovid's interest in the narrative potential of the simile, see Boyd 1997, 90–131.

35. For a detailed exploration of the relationship between Daedalus' labyrinth and the narrative of the *Metamorphoses,* among other things, see Boyd 2006.

REFERENCES

Anderson, R. J., P. J. Parsons, and R. G. M. Nisbet. 1979. "Elegiacs by Gallus from Qaṣr Ibrîm." *Journal of Roman Studies* 69: 125–55.

Barchiesi, Alessandro. 1997. *The Poet and the Prince: Ovid and Augustan Discourse.* Berkeley, Los Angeles, and London: University of California Press. [= 1994. *Il poeta e il principe: Ovidio e il discorso Augusteo.* Rome and Bari: Laterza.]

Boyd, Barbara Weiden. 1997. *Ovid's Literary Loves: Influence and Innovation in the Amores.* Ann Arbor: University of Michigan Press.

———. 2000. "*Celabitur auctor:* The Crisis of Authority and Narrative Patterning in Ovid *Fasti* 5." *Phoenix* 54: 64–98.

———. 2003. "*Itala nam tellus Graecia maior erat:* 'Poetic Syncretism' and the Divinities of Ovid, *Fasti* 4." *Mouseion* 3: 13–35.

————. 2006. "Two Rivers and the Reader in Ovid, *Metamorphoses* 8."
   Transactions of the American Philological Association 136: 73–108.

Cahoon, Leslie 1988. "The Bed as Battlefield: Erotic Conquest and
   Military Metaphor in Ovid's *Amores.*" *Transactions of the American Philological Association* 118: 293–307.

Claassen, Jo-Marie. 1999. *Displaced Persons: The Literature of Exile
   from Cicero to Boethius.* Madison: University of Wisconsin Press.

Crabbe, Anna. 1981. "Structure and Content in Ovid's 'Metamorphoses.'"
   Aufstieg und Niedergang der römischen Welt 2.31.4: 2274–327.

Fairweather, Janet. 1984. "The 'Gallus Papyrus': A New Interpretation."
   Classical Quarterly 34.1: 167–74.

Fantham, R. Elaine. 1985. "Ovid, Germanicus and the Composition of
   the *Fasti.*" *Proceedings of the Liverpool Latin Seminar* 5: 243–81.

————. 1992. "Ceres, Liber, and Flora: Georgic and Anti-Georgic
   Elements in Ovid's *Fasti.*" *Proceedings of the Cambridge Philological Society* 38: 39–56.

————. 1995. "Recent Readings of Ovid's *Fasti.*" *Classical Philology*
   90: 367–78.

————, ed. 1998. *Ovid,* Fasti *Book IV.* Cambridge: Cambridge University Press.

Farrell, Joseph. 2001. *Latin Language and Latin Culture from Ancient
   to Modern Times.* Cambridge: Cambridge University Press.

Fitton Brown, A. D. 1985. "The Unreality of Ovid's Tomitan Exile."
   Liverpool Classical Monthly 10.2: 18–22.

Goold, G. P. 1965. "Amatoria Critica." *Harvard Studies in Classical
   Philology* 69: 1–107.

Greene, Ellen. 1998. *The Erotics of Domination: Male Desire and the
   Mistress in Latin Love Poetry.* Baltimore, Md.: Johns Hopkins
   University Press.

Hardie, Philip R. 1993. *The Epic Successors of Virgil: A Study in the
   Dynamics of a Tradition.* Cambridge: Cambridge University Press.

Herbert-Brown, Geraldine. 1994. *Ovid and the* Fasti: *An Historical
   Study.* Oxford: Clarendon Press.

————, ed. 2002. *Ovid's* Fasti: *Historical Readings at Its Bimillen-
   nium.* Oxford: Oxford University Press.

Hershkowitz, Debra. 1998. *Valerius Flaccus' Argonautica: Abbreviated Voyages in Silver Latin Epic.* Oxford: Clarendon Press.

Hinds, Stephen. 1987. "Generalising about Ovid." *Ramus* 16: 4–31. [= A. J. Boyle, ed., *The Imperial Muse: Ramus Essays on Roman Literature of the Empire,* 4–31. Victoria, Australia: Aureal Publications.]

Hollis, Adrian S., ed. 1970. *Ovid,* Metamorphoses *Book VIII.* Oxford: Clarendon Press.

Holzberg, N. 1998. *"Ter quinque volumina* as *carmen perpetuum:* The Division into Books in Ovid's *Metamorphoses." Materiali e discussioni per l'analisi dei testi classici* 40: 77–98.

Kenney, E. J. 2002. "Ovid's Language and Style." In B. W. Boyd, ed., *Brill's Companion to Ovid,* 27–89. Leiden, Boston, and Cologne: Brill.

Knox, P. E. 1984. "Sappho Fr. 31 LP and Catullus 51: A Suggestion." *Quaderni Urbinati di Cultura Classica* 46: 97–102.

McKeown, J. C., ed. 1987, 1989, 1998, —. *Ovid,* Amores: *Text, Prolegomena and Commentary.* 4 vols. Liverpool, Wolfeboro, N.H., and Leeds: F. Cairns.

Miller, John F., ed. 1985. *Ovid,* Fasti *II.* Bryn Mawr, Pa.: Bryn Mawr College.

Nagle, Betty Rose, ed. 1996. *Ovid,* Fasti *V.* Bryn Mawr, Pa.: Bryn Mawr College.

Newlands, Carole. 1995. *Playing with Time: Ovid and the* Fasti. Ithaca, N.Y., and London: Cornell University Press.

Ogilvie, Robert M., ed. 1965. *A Commentary on Livy, Books 1–5.* Oxford: Clarendon Press.

Otis, Brooks. 1970. *Ovid as an Epic Poet.* 2nd ed. Cambridge: Cambridge University Press.

Platnauer, Maurice. 1951. *Latin Elegiac Verse: A Study of the Metrical Usages of Tibullus, Propertius & Ovid.* Cambridge: Cambridge University Press.

Sedley, David N. 1998. *Lucretius and the Transformation of Greek Wisdom.* Cambridge: Cambridge University Press.

Thibault, John C. 1964. *The Mystery of Ovid's Exile.* Berkeley and Los Angeles: University of California Press.

Tissol, Garth. 2002. "The House of Fame: Roman History and Augustan Politics in *Metamorphoses* 11–15." In B. W. Boyd, ed., *Brill's Companion to Ovid,* 305–35. Leiden, Boston, and Cologne: Brill.

Watson, Patricia. 2002. "*Praecepta amoris:* Ovid's Didactic Elegy." In B. W. Boyd, ed., *Brill's Companion to Ovid,* 141–65. Leiden, Boston, and Cologne: Brill.

White, Peter. 2002. "Ovid and the Augustan Milieu." In B. W. Boyd, ed., *Brill's Companion to Ovid,* 1–25. Leiden, Boston, and Cologne: Brill.

CHAPTER 3

"Tensile Horace"
Negotiating Critical Boundaries

Ronnie Ancona

We tend, when we teach, to rely on how we were taught—either imitating our former teachers and their approaches or sometimes revolting against them. In either case, what informs our current teaching is often out of date. When we are pressed for time (as all teachers are, but secondary school teachers are perhaps especially so) or when we leave behind our formal academic training, it can be difficult to stay current with classical scholarship. Thus we may experience a lag in our awareness of new work in our field. It is my hope in this essay to show some of the exciting work that is being done on Horace (in relation to the *Odes* in particular, since they are most widely taught) in order to refashion the sense of Horace that teachers may have from their student days.

Many people do not like reading the *Odes* very much.[1] Why? Let me suggest some reasons based on initial reactions to the *Odes* that I have seen in students of my own, reactions I have surmised from the reading of Catullus and Horace answers for the Advanced Placement Latin exams, as well as notions about the *Odes* that I think still prevail in much of the classics profession, particularly among those who have not had reason to keep up on some of the more recent scholarship on Horace. After reading Catullus (and this is how students are typically introduced to Horace, whether through AP courses in high school or through

53

Latin Lyric classes in college), many find Horace dry, unemotional, and difficult to read. And when he is finally "figured out," he seems clichéd—a detached old pontificator spewing out "words of wisdom" from his distanced stance. The reasons for these reactions are, I think, perfectly understandable. The impression of dryness and lack of emotion is grounded in the distanced pose that the speaker in the *Odes* frequently maintains. He assumes a detached position that makes him seem like an uninvolved commentator upon his world. And the "advice" he gives and the "conclusions" he appears to draw often do not strike us as particularly profound (*carpe diem* "seize the day," etc.). In addition, the difficulties in teaching Horace are real. And if the rewards for reading him seem minimal, then the effort does not seem worth it. One of the difficulties is the fact that the "subject matter" of the *Odes* is difficult to pin down. Just when a poem seems to be "about" one thing, it goes off in another direction to be "about" something else. So even making simple statements about the "content" of the *Odes* may cause a problem. Then there is the difficulty of reading (or translating) them. My guess is that if one has ever taught Catullus and then plunged into Horace, one will have found students somewhat overwhelmed. Horace's "literariness," as manifested, for example, in his incredibly flexible use of word order, as well as his indirect allusions, can be forbidding.

Of course, seeing Catullus as the "opposite" of all that I have just said about Horace would be a naive way of viewing him, just as seeing Horace solely in the terms I have given above would, I hope to show, be naive, too, for Catullus can also be complex, highly allusive, and emotionally detached (such as when he separates himself from his own emotions through self-address, as in Poem 8: *Miser Catulle, desinas ineptire . . .*).[2] Nevertheless, many a student will approach Catullus, and even be encouraged by his or her teacher to do so, as the emotionally immediate, spontaneous, truly "lyric" poet. If a teacher shares the view of Horace that I have outlined above, as a dry, emotionless giver of advice, I doubt that students will find him of much interest, and they will probably attribute the teacher's interest in him (if there is any) to the teacher's advanced (and therefore probably "unsexy") age.

What I hope to show is that this traditional view of Horace as the detached, unemotional (if wry) old commentator sending forth clichés can be challenged by paying close attention to how Horace himself undermines this characterization. If we explore the "tensions" in his work that make such a characterization too easy (and new scholarship on Horace will help us to do this), a far more interesting poet will emerge for teachers and students alike.

Most Horatian scholars see as central to Horace's literary project a poetics that is constituted by various "tensions" surrounding issues of literary, social, and historical "negotiation." That is to say, Horace's poetics involves a maneuvering around and through—a creation of tensions about—various issues rather than some simple statement about them. These issues include the nature of the lyric genre and Horace's relationship to Augustus. This "tensile" character of Horace's writing seems to have been and to still be a constant in Horatian scholarship.[3] This essay explores how some of these tensions are played out in newer approaches to Horace.

I have chosen to take as my focal point a poem that I think will successfully allow for exploration of these tensions in the context of recent Horatian scholarship. It is not my intention to argue here for any particular or exclusive reading of that poem, but rather to use it as a vehicle for engaging with that new scholarship. The poem I will use, *Odes* 1.37, the so-called Cleopatra Ode, is part of the Advanced Placement Latin Literature syllabus for Horace and is frequently taught in college Latin classes. In addition, it is often cited or used in translation in Roman history or Roman civilization classes for addressing the politics of the Augustan Age. I hope to show in the context of this poem how recent scholarly work can be readily understood, and in turn how the reading of the poem can be expanded or enriched through an awareness of recent critical perspectives.

One may ask: Why share recent critical perspectives about
Horace, or other authors, with students who are still just learning
how to read Latin? My emphatic answer is that since reading
(both in Latin and in English), thinking, and writing create a kind
of synergistic energy, each activity serves to enhance the other.
To anticipate our discussion by giving a small example from
Odes 1.37, a discussion of gender issues in Horatian criticism
might make a student, for example, remember the Latin words
mulier and *muliebriter* more successfully than a teaching approach
that considered such discussion beyond the scope of the student's
abilities. And from the opposite perspective, knowing those Latin
words makes the student better able to read and understand critical writing. Creating better "Latin readers," a goal shared by all
Latin teachers, means more than teaching just grammar and
syntax. It involves teaching intellectual context and interpretive
techniques as well as the wider context in which those interpretations are situated.

It will be helpful to have handy for our discussion Horace's
poem in Latin as well as a literal translation:

Odes 1.37

Nunc est bibendum, nunc pede libero
pulsanda tellus, nunc Saliaribus
    ornare pulvinar deorum
        tempus erat dapibus, sodales.
antehac nefas depromere Caecubum   5
cellis avitis, dum Capitolio
    regina dementis ruinas
        funus et imperio parabat
contaminato cum grege turpium
morbo virorum, quidlibet inpotens   10
    sperare fortunaque dulci
        ebria; sed minuit furorem
vix una sospes navis ab ignibus,
mentemque lymphatam Mareotico

redegit in veros timores 15
    Caesar ab Italia volantem
remis adurgens, accipiter velut
mollis columbas aut leporem citus
    venator in campis nivalis
    Haemoniae, daret ut catenis 20
fatale monstrum, quae generosius
perire quaerens nec muliebriter
    expavit ensem, nec latentis
    classe cita reparavit oras,
ausa et iacentem visere regiam 25
voltu sereno, fortis et asperas
    tractare serpentes, ut atrum
    corpore combiberet venenum,
deliberata morte ferocior:
saevis Liburnis scilicet invidens 30
    privata deduci superbo
    non humilis mulier triumpho.[4]

Now it is necessary to drink, now it is necessary to beat the ground with unrestrained dance, now the time is overdue, companions, to adorn the couch of the gods with Salian feasts. Before this it was a sacrilege to bring out the Caecuban wine from the ancestral cellars, while a queen was preparing mad ruin for the Capitolium and destruction for the government with her foul flock of men shameful in their disease, wild enough to hope for anything and drunk with sweet fortune; but scarcely one ship safe from the fires weakened her frenzy, and Caesar drove back her mind distracted with Mareotic wine into real fears, pressing hard upon her with his oars as she flew from Italy, just as the hawk (pursues) gentle doves or the swift hunter a hare on the fields of snowy Thessaly, so that he could give the deadly marvel to chains. She, seeking to perish more nobly, did not in womanish manner fear the sword and did not reach hidden shores with her swift fleet. And she dared to look at her ruined palace with calm face, brave, also, to handle fierce snakes in order to drink completely with her body the black poison, more bold because of her carefully considered death; refusing, evidently, to be led back to Rome as a private citizen by cruel galleys for a proud triumphal procession—a not humble woman.[5]

I include here the introductory material I wrote for *Odes* 1.37 in my textbook *Horace: Selected Odes and Satire 1.9*. It is intended to give some basic background on this ode for student and teacher without suggesting a particular interpretation of the poem. It is written to raise issues and questions rather than to give answers. The accompanying guide for teachers intentionally does not provide answers to these kinds of open-ended questions, for it is hoped that the questions will provoke independent thought among teachers as well.

The historical context for this ode is the defeat of Octavian's enemy, Cleopatra VII of Egypt, at the battle of Actium off the west coast of Greece in 31 B.C.E. Cleopatra and Antony were the final obstacles standing in the way of Octavian's total power. After their defeat at Actium, Antony and Cleopatra returned to Alexandria, Egypt. When their land forces were defeated and Octavian entered Alexandria, both committed suicide. The fact that Horace does not mention Antony in the poem helps to portray the conflict not as a civil war, but rather as a foreign threat.

The endings of Horace's odes are frequently a source of interest (and sometimes of surprise). In this ode Horace follows five stanzas of celebration about the defeat of a *fatale monstrum* with an extended evocation in the last three stanzas of Cleopatra's nobility in the face of defeat. What are we to make of this? Does this express ambivalence on the part of Horace about Octavian's defeat of his final obstacle to complete rule? Or does it make Octavian's conquest all the more outstanding because of the notable dignity of the one he has conquered?[6]

Now let us see how we might relate the Horatian tensions addressed in current scholarship to our reading of the poem. While there is an extensive bibliography specifically on the Cleopatra Ode, my goal here is not to present scholarship narrowly focused on the poem, but rather to discuss recent book-length treatments of Horace (some of which discuss this ode, some of which do not) in the context of the ode. My purpose is to open up to the readers of this book some broad, overarching, new approaches to Horace that can then be utilized in the classroom not just with one poem, but with many. Rather than make the reader an expert on the scholarship particular to *Odes* 1.37, I want to help the reader see what issues are being addressed in current Horatian scholarship, and thus to prepare him or her to approach the *Odes* in general with some new thinking and teaching tools. I have chosen to discuss six recent books with differing perspectives that focus on one or another aspect of Horace, but that taken together will provide readers with a wealth of material for further developing the teaching of the *Odes*. While of course I cannot do justice to any of these books in a few pages of discussion (and I recommend that the readers of this book read any or all of them in their entirety), I hope to show how various perspectives from new scholarship on Horace can be incorporated into the classroom without much difficulty. While book-length treatments of Horace may seem daunting to the busy classroom teacher, the effort required to introduce "something" of this new work to students is not as great as it might seem. If my summary of portions of the arguments from these books is in some way useful to the classroom teacher of Horace, I will have met my goal.

The following books are to be discussed: Gregson Davis, *Polyhymnia: The Rhetoric of Horatian Discourse;* Michèle Lowrie, *Horace's Narrative Odes;* Ellen Oliensis, *Horace and the Rhetoric of Authority;* Michael Putnam, *Horace's* Carmen Saeculare; Ronnie Ancona, *Time and the Erotic in Horace's* Odes; and Phebe Lowell Bowditch, *Horace and the Gift Economy of Patronage.* Some are very recent; none is more than about a decade and a half old. It is likely, then, that readers of this book who have been teaching for a long time were not exposed to these books when they themselves were in school. In addition, newer teachers may also be unfamiliar with them, for it is not uncommon for Latin teachers to have read the Latin, perhaps with a commentary, but to have read little in the area of secondary scholarship. The "tensile" quality of Horace that I discussed at the beginning of this essay and with which some older Horatian scholarship concerned itself is a common thread running through the new scholarship discussed here.[7] How that tensile quality takes shape, though, differs from book to book, from scholar to scholar, and it is in that difference that various perspectives on Horace become apparent. The key notions that I hope the reader will take away from these books to utilize in the classroom are the following: "lyric as political negotiator" (Davis and Lowrie), "face" and "authority and deference" (Oliensis), "conditionality" (Putnam), "power and desire" (Ancona), and "gift economy" (Bowditch). While these notions—even some of the terms themselves—may seem opaque at first to the novice at Horatian secondary scholarship, they can be made accessible and useful to the teacher of Horace, despite their seeming (or real) complexity.

The generic tensions, constraints, and rhetorical strategies of lyric have been addressed in elegant fashion by Gregson Davis and Michèle Lowrie. Their approaches share an interest in how Horace allows his lyric to incorporate and rework themes and strategies beyond the expected purview of the lyric genre.[8] They are both interested in the rhetorical strategies of lyric. As my textbook introduction to *Odes* 1.37 cited above makes clear, there are distinct tensions operating in the poem, and virtually any critic will somehow have to address them. Davis addresses one of the tensions in the poem—that of praise and dispraise— and argues that "Despite the prominence accorded to Cleopatra in the narrative, the oblique rhetorical agenda is praise of the ruler whose name appears at the precise midpoint of the poem" (235). Praise of the vanquished Cleopatra enhances Octavian, the one who has brought about her defeat. Davis utilizes conventional praise material from Horace's archaic Greek lyric predecessor and model, Pindar, to argue that the agency of Octavian in Cleopatra's transformation secures his role as *laudandus* or "one to be praised." He further articulates how the banqueting, partying motif, connected with the desire to escape from the knowledge of mortality, shows the Romans as the appropriately controlled celebrants and Cleopatra as the one lacking in proper decorum. If Cleopatra sobers up and gains stature at the end of the poem, this, in turn, shows the transformative power of Octavian. Davis does not deny the poem's tensions, but rather argues that an examination of the way Horace uses conventional material— Pindaric praise poetry and the theme of the symposium—helps us to situate his rhetorical point.

Lowrie's interest in this poem, unlike Davis', lies less with its specific rhetorical strategy than with Horace's ability to contain narrative within lyric, which in contemporary usage is often opposed to narrative and drama, or to expand lyric to encompass narrative. She is particularly successful at addressing how the historical narrative in Horace is shaped by the genre of lyric. Thus her approach is a welcome antidote to one that might try to merely pull historical "facts" out of the poems. Lowrie's book is, in a sense, a successor to Davis', for Davis charts a number of paths for seeing how Horace incorporates nonlyric into lyric. For example, he discusses Horace's use of the *recusatio* or "refusal" to in fact write about a particular topic about which he says he refuses to write.[9] In similar fashion, for Lowrie, in the narrative odes, Horace manages to "tell a story," but it is one that is shaped by the nonnarrative devices of lyric, for instance, by temporal compression, by which "[t]wo years, 31 and 30 BC, condense into three scenes (threat, conflict and chase, defeat)," and Octavian's triumph of 29 seems to follow immediately upon the death of Cleopatra (144). Of course, historical background is essential to understanding a poem such as this, but Lowrie would argue that Horace here and elsewhere is creating his own lyric history, which is quite distinct from the historical record. While Lowrie somewhat hesitantly still sees the poem as praising Caesar (as does Davis), she is very attracted to the figure of Cleopatra as both Same and Other, drunk and sober, ignoble Easterner and Stoic Roman choosing death, Woman and not-Woman. Lowrie focuses on the ways in which the poem suppresses the issue of civil war (the opponent becomes Cleopatra and foreign, while Antony, the Roman civil opponent, is suppressed), only to refigure it through displacement onto Cleopatra. That is to say, the tensions surrounding Cleopatra and the transformation she undergoes in the poem make it impossible, according to Lowrie, to see her only as enemy, only as foreigner, only as Eastern female drunk. For Lowrie, Cleopatra complicates Octavian's victory.

Ellen Oliensis approaches Horace biographically, not in the perhaps more familiar sense of creating a life out of his poems, but rather in the sense of exploring the "life" that lives in the poems. More specifically, using the notion of "face," that is, "the public, projected self-image that is the basic currency of social interactions" (1), she examines Horace's gestures of deference and authority. "Authority makes a claim for the poet's face; deference pays tribute to the face of the audience(s)" (3). She makes the important argument that it is difficult for Horace's authority and Augustus' authority to occupy the same space, and that praise of Augustus is often made possible by his semi-exclusion. For Oliensis, Horace's resistance to closure, a hallmark of his style, is connected with his carving out of a space for authorial assertion. Thus, the end of *Odes* 1.37 "may express Horace's impulse to create a space, over against the space now occupied by Caesar, for the exercise of his own power, his own lyric fortitude" (145). The poet who calls himself *princeps* in *Odes* 3.30 triumphs in the poetic sphere as the pattern is being established in the political sphere for military triumphs to be celebrated only by Augustus and the imperial family. Thus, while Davis sees Horace's rhetorical strategies as ultimately serving the purpose of praise of Octavian, and Lowrie sees the historically transformative power of lyric creating an uneasy and incomplete suppression of civil war through the paradoxical figure of Cleopatra, Oliensis sees a triumph for the poet in the poem.

If one figure in Horatian scholarship were to stand out as advocate of Horace triumphing throughout his poetry, it would probably be Michael Putnam, who sees Horace's art and poetic powers as "an artifice of eternity."[10] This is one reason why his recent book *Horace's* Carmen Saeculare, an elaborate and nuanced discussion of the *carmen saeculare,* the ode written by Horace at Augustus' request for public performance by a chorus of young boys and girls at the Ludi Saeculares or Secular Games of 17 B.C.E., is of particular interest. It addresses the issue of how a poet can negotiate the boundaries between celebrating a political/public event and maintaining his distance and power as the one who enables the commemoration. How does a critic who sees Horace's art as triumphantly transcendent deal with Horace's writing of a poem for a particular public, religious, political context? Part of the answer lies in Putnam's discussion of the poem as transitional—between the more detached, private poet of *Odes* Books 1–3 and a more civically engaged poet who has come to support (albeit conditionally) the Augustan rule that becomes a reality several years after the battle of Actium. For Putnam, the *carmen saeculare* becomes a site for analysis of Horace's path toward the communal acknowledgment of his poetic powers, desired in his earlier work and later found. He argues that Horace's suppression of the "I" or "self" in service of communal song is only partial in the *carmen saeculare.* For example, Horace's description of the performing chorus of the poem as *doctus* or "taught" shifts attention back to that "self" by bringing to mind the poet, the guiding author behind the words of praise and celebration. According to Putnam, Horace's acceptance of the commission to write the *carmen saeculare* "is to turn the metaphor of *c.* 3.30 into reality: Horace will now literally share in a major moment of the state religion and become a type of priest" (49–50). Yet for Putnam, this does not represent a capitulation to Augustus. Rather, "the ultimate power rests not with Augustan military, political, or even ethical prowess, however worthy of applause, but with the poet who in singing of them confirms their quality" (50). "However striking his accomplishment may be as inspiration for song, it is Augustus who is finally beholden to his poet, not vice versa" (50).

For the teacher of *Odes* 1.37, Putnam's approach is useful in outlining the political/literary path by which a partial outsider such as Horace becomes embedded in the culture of the political and literary elite while maintaining his own poetic voice. Like Lowrie and Oliensis, Putnam is interested in Horace's negotiation of space for himself within his lyric discourse. In teaching about the ambiguous and shifting portrayal of Cleopatra in *Odes* 1.37, one might use Putnam's notion of a "conditional" relationship with Octavian/Augustus to explain how and why Horace might veer away from unconditional celebration of the victory at Actium.

Despite my specific focus on the erotic, in particular, my argument in *Time and the Erotic in Horace's Odes* shares the more general Horatian scholarly concern with space for the self within lyric discourse. I argue that the frequently detached, ironic stance of the poet/lover contains an indirectly expressed and transgressive desire to control the temporality and autonomy of the beloved. Just as Oliensis, for example, focuses on the difficulty of Augustus and Horace occupying the same "potent" position at one time, I argue that Horace's detached, ironic love discourse typically attempts to force the object of desire out of a "subject" position, leaving only the poet/lover in the position of control. The "split" rhetoric of the detached voice that contains covert desire often takes shape through a conflict between the literal sense of the language and its figurative power in the erotic odes. For example, in *Odes* 1.23, the literal message is "Don't be afraid," but the figurative language of predatory pursuit suggests that Chloe has much to fear.[11] Here, in the Cleopatra Ode, such an analysis can help us complicate the dynamics of power between male and female, between pursuer and pursued. Just as Horace's apparent strategy in *Odes* 1.23 might be defined as "seduction" but his figurative strategy as "control," in the Cleopatra Ode the ostensible strategy may be to praise Octavian's success at Actium, while the figurative effect of the poem's conclusion leaves us with a *non humilis mulier* (a not humble woman) who evades Octavian's triumph and creates her own. In fact, one could look at Cleopatra as an object of Octavian's desire who escapes his attempt at control. Her escape into controlled, sober, mannish, individual action inscribes her, still as woman, into the "subject" position of a male Roman discourse of power, displacing Octavian, the initial "subject" of desire.

While my approach based on *Time and the Erotic* focuses on the "space" demanded by the desiring subject or self, it shares with all of the approaches mentioned above a concern with negotiating boundaries, be they between history and lyric, poetry and politics, or self and other. The last Horatian scholar I will discuss has perhaps the broadest approach in terms of her interest in Horace's poetry as a kind of negotiation. Phebe Lowell Bowditch, in *Horace and the Gift Economy of Patronage,* explores the material and social conditions and practices that form the context for Horace's poetry. As her book title suggests, Bowditch focuses on the "gift economy" of patronage or friendship. She argues that "[t]he concept of the 'gift' . . . brings into focus this particular dynamic by which the social relations defining Horace's experience of literary patronage at once determine and are reflexively modified by his poems" (7). The gift of the Sabine Farm (for which she acknowledges that the evidence is not definitive)[12] becomes for Bowditch a locus of "symbolic benefaction" wherein the material and exploitative elements of gift giving and their concomitant debts are in part transformed by Horace into the aestheticized source of his voluntary production of poetry (26). This is a difficult and exciting book. Bowditch's approach forces the reader to see *Odes* 1.37 in the wider context of a "gift economy." That is to say, what does it mean for Horace to write a poem about the battle of Actium? Has he incurred obligations that then produce a poem of this sort? Or is this sort of poem an enactment of Horace's freedom from obligation? Is his poem a "gift," and if so, of what sort and for whom? How does his autonomy and independence as a poet figure in what sort of gift "in return" he wants to or can produce?

What I have called the "tensile" quality of Horace can take many forms. Genre, politics, gender, and social status are all boundaries that Horace plays with transgressing. His "tensile" art allows him to shift positions, to avoid categorization even when his images—such as those of Cleopatra in *Odes* 1.37— take on a certain specificity that then transmutes into another specificity. Each of the Horatian scholars whose books I have discussed approaches this "tensile" quality in a different fashion. Davis' attention to the way in which Horace uses conventional lyric praise and dispraise to negotiate a political position, Lowrie's focus on the political implications of Horace's writing of "lyric" narrative, Oliensis' use of the concept of "face" to help define Horace's relationships, Putnam's foregrounding of the poet's triumph, Ancona's of the relation of gender to power and desire, and Bowditch's exploration of the consequences of the "gift" all allow for new and different ways of reading and teaching *Odes* 1.37, and Horace's poems more generally. If one teaches Horace, should one now feel obligated to read *all* of these books in their entirety? Not necessarily. I would argue, though, that using just one or two of the approaches mentioned here will allow the teacher to create a "window" for his or her students into Horace's *Odes*. And then the teacher can take class time to argue about what that particular "window" allows one to see (or not see).

NOTES

1. I discussed some of the negative notions about Horace in "Disruptive Desire: Sexuality, Gender and the Interpretation of Horace's

Odes," a paper delivered in 1995 at the American Philological Association/
American Classical League joint session "New Approaches to Teaching
the Odes of Horace."

    2. See William Fitzgerald's contribution to this volume on Catul-
lus' complexity.

    3. I draw my title and its use of the word "tensile" (capable of
tension) and its related notion of "tensile strength" (the greatest stress
in width that a substance can undergo without breaking) from Alwin
Nikolais' signature dance piece, "Tensile Involvement" (1953), which
I saw performed in my childhood. Its use of elastic ribbons attached to
dancers' bodies and its attendant spectacle of kinetic power moved me
then and taught me a new word. By calling Horace "tensile" in this essay,
I hope to suggest the elastic, expansive characteristic of his work,
which allows for tensions that are held and reconfigured and held
again. I suspect that some of my interest in Horace's poetry is not
unrelated to my early interest in modern dance. Horace keeps things
"in motion" despite the seeming fixedness of the written word.

    4. From Borzsák, *Horatius: Opera.*

    5. Ancona 1999, 2005b, 45.

    6. Ancona 1999, 2005a, 55.

    7. See, e.g., Steele Commager's excellent book *The Odes of Horace*,
published originally in 1962 by Yale University Press, and reprinted
by University of Oklahoma Press with additional material by David
Armstrong. Commager's work, arising out of New Criticism, anticipates
several of the notions addressed in this essay, such as Horace's shifts
of thought, complex authorial voice, and ambivalence about Augustus.
My own work on Horace, despite its taking issue at times with Commager, is deeply indebted to him. For a brief discussion of Commager's
contribution to Horatian scholarship, see Armstrong's foreword.

    8. There is no simple definition of "lyric." For the Greeks and
Romans, a lyric originally meant a song composed for the lyre; however, by Roman times, with its written culture, that "song" would have
become metaphorical. In addition, lyric was often seen as metrically
defined, i.e., those poems written in particular "lyric" meters. Miller
1994 has argued that what we think of today as lyric did not exist
until a largely written culture allowed for a self-reflexive subjectivity to

develop, and that Catullus therefore is "lyric" in a modern sense, while Sappho is not. Miller's argument, whether or not one finds it convincing, points to the important issue of the culturally specific material conditions and circumstances of poetic composition and performance. Abrams 1999, 146, provides the following: "In the most common use of the term, a lyric is any fairly short poem, consisting of the utterance by a single speaker, who expresses a state of mind or a process of perception, thought, and feeling."

9. See, e.g., Davis 1991, 33–34 and 36–39, on *Odes* 1.6.

10. See the title of his 1986 book, *Artifices of Eternity: Horace's Fourth Book of Odes*.

11. For a full discussion of *Odes* 1.23, see Ancona 1994, 70–74. An earlier version of that discussion appears in Ancona 1989.

12. Bowditch 2001, 4, takes the position that "the literary evidence suggests that Maecenas . . . gave Horace his celebrated 'Sabine Farm.'" She cites the relevant sources for gift and date: "the comments of Porphyrio and Pseudo-Acro on *Epodes* 1.31 and *Odes* 2.18.12–14, and the implications of *Satires* 2.6" (4 n. 9). However, she states, 118n.6, that not all support this view, and that Augustus has been suggested as the source of the farm. Mankin 1995, 61, is skeptical of the assumption that Maecenas is the source of the farm and writes on *Epodes* 1.31–32: "In fact, he is quite vague as to how M. [Maecenas] has 'enriched' him." Mankin 1995, 2n.13, further says: "It is often stated that H. owed his 'Sabine farm' . . . to Maecenas, but neither he nor Suetonius says this. It seems an inference from *C.* 2.18.12–14 . . . , which is usually taken to mean 'now that he has given me a Sabine estate, I need ask nothing from my powerful friend' (= Maecenas . . .). But the passage makes more sense in its context if H. is saying 'Since I have an estate that belongs to me [i.e. makes me independent], I do not have to ask anything from a powerful friend.'"

REFERENCES

Abrams, M. H. 1999. 7th ed. *A Glossary of Literary Terms*. Fort Worth, Tex.: Harcourt Brace.

Ancona, Ronnie. 1989. "The Subterfuge of Reason: Horace *Odes* 1.23 and the Construction of Male Desire." *Helios* 16:49–57. Reprinted in Anderson 1999, 63–72.

———. 1994. *Time and the Erotic in Horace's Odes*. Durham, N.C.: Duke University Press.

———. 1999. 2nd ed., 2005a. *Horace: Selected Odes and Satire 1.9*. Wauconda, Ill.: Bolchazy-Carducci Publishers.

———. 1999. 2nd ed., 2005b. *Horace: Selected Odes and Satire 1.9— Teacher's Guide*. Wauconda, Ill.: Bolchazy-Carducci Publishers.

Anderson, William, ed. 1999. *Why Horace? A Collection of Interpretations*. Wauconda, Ill.: Bolchazy-Carducci Publishers.

Borsák, Stephanus, ed. 1984. *Horatius: Opera*. Leipzig.

Bowditch, Phebe Lowell. 2001. *Horace and the Gift Economy of Patronage*. Berkeley: University of California Press.

Commager, Steele. 1995. *The Odes of Horace*. Norman: University of Oklahoma Press.

Davis, Gregson. 1991. *Polyhymnia: The Rhetoric of Horatian Discourse*. Berkeley: University of California Press.

Lowrie, Michéle. 1997. *Horace's Narrative Odes*. Oxford: Clarendon Press.

Mankin, David. 1995. *Horace:* Epodes. Cambridge: Cambridge University Press.

Miller, Paul Allen. 1994. *Lyric Texts and Lyric Consciousness: The Birth of a Genre From Archaic Greece To Augustan Rome*. New York: Routledge.

Oliensis, Ellen. 1998. *Horace and the Rhetoric of Authority*. Cambridge: Cambridge University Press.

Putnam, Michael. 1986. *Artifices of Eternity: Horace's Fourth Book of Odes*. Ithaca, N.Y.: Cornell University Press.

———. 2000. *Horace's* Carmen Saeculare. New Haven, Conn.: Yale University Press.

CHAPTER 4

CICERONIAN SCHOLARSHIP IN THE LATIN CLASSROOM

James M. May

The relative merits of Cicero's oratorical style were a matter of debate even in his own time and among his own contemporaries. The answers to his critics that he personally supplied in, for example, his *Brutus* and *Orator* were, of course, only a prelude to those that supporters and apologists would continue to offer over the course of two millennia following his death.[1] And while the study of and devotion to Ciceronian oratory has certainly waxed and waned at various times and under various circumstances over that long course of time, it is perhaps remarkable that for scholars and experts interested in rhetoric and oratory, as well as for students pursuing some fluency in the venerable language of the ancient Romans, Cicero's speeches still stand as models of both effective verbal persuasion and elegant Latin prose. For admirers of Cicero, this is, to be sure, as it should be; for beyond the fact that his extant corpus of writings is a huge one that stands as a veritable gold mine of information about one of the most interesting periods in all of Roman history, the truth remains that Rome's finest speaker was, to put it simply, very good at what he did: his talent at persuading an audience has been matched by few orators in history, and his mastery of prose style and expression, in spite of criticism from "Atticists" both ancient and modern,[2] stands nearly unrivaled. In recognition of

71

these facts, it is likely that many students enrolled in advanced Latin courses in the United States will, for the foreseeable future, have at least some contact with Cicero during their years of studying the language.

Those of us who teach in the high school or undergraduate Latin classroom certainly realize that the vast majority of our time and effort must be devoted to helping our students merely to read and understand what Cicero has to say and how he says it in the original Latin text. Just as the rhythm, beauty, and power of the Vergilian hexameter cannot fully be appreciated in an English translation, so the rhythm, beauty, and power of Ciceronian prose cannot be grasped in all its dimensions through translation. But while solid knowledge of Latin grammar and syntax is a necessary first step in tackling a Ciceronian oration, such a foundation is actually only the means by which we achieve the greater goal of understanding and appreciating not only the verbal and stylistic virtues of a speech, but also its historical and social context—not to mention the particular rhetorical strategies that the orator employs in it in order to persuade his audience. Indeed, these are the aspects of a speech that students often find most intriguing; they can provide the interest and incentive to study a Ciceronian oration with genuine enthusiasm. While some areas of scholarly pursuit are too esoteric for introduction into the high school or undergraduate classroom, several others are quite accessible, and can provide an effective entrée for both teacher and student to approach Cicero's speeches in ways that will assist them greatly in their attempts to analyze and to gain an appreciation of Cicero's oratorical art.

Christopher Craig, in a recent article that discusses current trends in scholarly work on Cicero's rhetorica and speeches, has identified several topics and approaches that have characterized Ciceronian scholarship during the past twenty-five years.[3] Chief among these for our purposes are (1) the continuing debate about the relationship between spoken and published versions of the orations; (2) the analysis of a speech as a specific response to a specific rhetorical challenge, that is, as an act of progressive manipulation of the audience by the orator in order to win support for his case (so-called "persuasive-process criticism"); such analysis is often joined to a careful analysis of Cicero's application of argument based on character (*ethos*) as part of that process; and (3) the analysis of the contents of a speech from culturally specific Roman points of view. In the elaborations that follow, I borrow extensively from Professor Craig's fine account, which I commend to anyone who is interested in a more detailed, comprehensive treatment.

Everyone who is even remotely familiar with the corpus of extant Ciceronian oratory knows that Cicero published speeches that he had never actually delivered. The five speeches that make up the second action of the *Verrines* represent orations that Cicero might have given, had the trial progressed to that stage. The "divine" *Second Philippic,* which reveals the unseemly side of Roman and Ciceronian invective in an all too graphic manner, was circulated as a pamphlet in response to an earlier attack upon Cicero by Mark Antony. Even for his speeches that we know were delivered in a court of law, evidence corroborates that differences sometimes existed between spoken and written versions. For example, the ancient commentator Asconius, writing on Cicero's celebrated speech in defense of Milo (who was charged with the murder of Publius Clodius), makes it clear that the speech Cicero actually delivered, while still in circulation, differed from the masterpiece on which he was commenting.[4] Some people at the time apparently suggested that the best defense of Milo would be to claim that Clodius' murder had been to the benefit of the state; but according to Asconius, Cicero eschewed that line of argument in his original spoken oration.[5] Milo was convicted in the ensuing trial and went into exile. Cicero subsequently sent to him a revised copy of the speech as we have it—which in fact contains (in sections 72–91) the argument that Clodius' death benefited the state. Upon receipt of the speech, Milo is reported to have quipped that he would never have had the opportunity to sample the mullets of Marseilles had Cicero delivered that version of the speech at the actual trial.[6] All of this would seem to confirm that the speech Cicero sent to him after the fact differed in some ways from the one he had delivered before Pompey, his armed guard, and the crowd in the Roman Forum. Thus, questions emerge not only about what Cicero might have actually said on a specific occasion in question, but also about how that version relates to the version of the speech published subsequently. Why were changes made, or, perhaps more important, why did Cicero choose to publish his speeches at all?

More than a quarter-century ago, Wilfried Stroh, rebutting Humbert's earlier theory that a published oration of Cicero was really a synthesis of various portions of the actual trial made by the orator after the fact,[7] argued forcefully that Cicero's primary motive for publication was to provide educational models of ways by which an orator might persuade a specific audience in a specific circumstance.[8] Although the published speech may deviate from the original spoken oration in detail, the published version nonetheless stands, in terms of arrangement, argument, and style, as an integral and valid act of persuasion, aimed by Cicero at convincing jurors in an actual court of law. While scholars have continued to temper and refine Stroh's approach, positing not just pedagogical but also political and self-promotional motives,[9] the general line of Stroh's argument seems to have taken hold among a majority of Ciceronian scholars today. Andrew Riggsby summarizes the position well:

> The direct evidence for relationship between the delivered and published versions of Cicero's speeches is weak. What there is suggests that most of the changes consist of small-scale stylistic polishing and occasional brief additions. There is little or no evidence for changes in the substance of any of Cicero's arguments. Stylistic details of the published speeches are characteristic of oral discourse; the simplest explanation for this is that

they derive directly from the original. A study of Cicero's implicit and explicit motivations for promulgating his speeches (advertising, information, and education) shows that it would have been to his advantage to reproduce fairly closely the texts of the speeches as he delivered them in court.[10]

The approach that has dominated scholarship dealing with Ciceronian oratory during the past quarter-century has undoubtedly been so-called "persuasive-process criticism," a mode of analysis that requires viewing a speech as the record of an oral process, aimed at persuading a particular audience in the context of a particular set of circumstances. Christopher Craig, himself a leading scholar of persuasive-process criticism, aptly describes it in this way:

> The speech represents an act of progressive manipulation in which every argument, word, and nuance moves towards the orator's persuasive goal. The fact that the orator must speak at all, that the audience is not already persuaded, indicates that there is some impediment to getting the audience to act or feel as he wants. This is the rhetorical challenge. The greater the rhetorical challenge overcome, the greater the success of the speech.[11]

Employing such a mode of criticism implies particular consequences. When one views the goal of a speech as persuasion at any price, certain assumptions may, in the interest of victory, have to be jettisoned. For example, while traditional rhetorical theory, the specific legal grounding of a case at issue, prevailing political circumstances, the actual guilt or innocence of a client, or even truth itself might, in theory, be expected to play a crucial role in an orator's speech on behalf of his client, in an actual case surrounded by real and extenuating circumstances, the manipulation of the audience or jury in order to gain support for the client

becomes foremost in the orator's eyes. Hence, it might be true
that election bribery (the charge lodged against L. Murena, consul-
elect for 62 B.C.) was a crime, and one deserving of punishment
in the state; yet in a state that stands threatened by the likes of a
Catiline, Cicero can play upon the psychology of the jury, through
wit, effective portrayal of character, and explosive arousal of
emotion, to convince them to wink at the formal charge of the case
in the interest of preserving the security of the state by starting the
new year with two consuls in office.[12] In such circumstances,
wherein truth can become a casualty to the manipulations of a
skillful speaker whose goal is to win his case, fascinating questions can be (and have been) posed concerning the relationship
between the orators and juries in Cicero's Rome, and the extent
to which the members of an audience might allow, or even
welcome, their own manipulation. In other words, were Roman
juries content to be entertained, to reward oratorical tours de
force with victories despite the guilt or innocence of the accused?
Zetzel, Riggsby, and Craig are among those who have addressed
this issue.[13]

Because persuasive process criticism is so intimately connected with the way the orator interacts with the audience and
with his attempt to persuade them in any specific circumstance,
it is natural that a great deal of recent Ciceronian scholarship
has concentrated on the ways in which Cicero depicts his own
character, his client's, his adversary's, as well as the characters
of others connected with the case at issue. The recognition by
George Kennedy and others of the widespread Roman practice
of advocacy[14] as well as the broader theoretical notions of *ethos* in
Cicero's own rhetorical works has laid the foundation for extremely
interesting work in this area, much of which is readily accessible
to both students and teachers of the speeches that are commonly
studied in the intermediate Latin classroom. Indeed, Cicero's effective portrayal of his own character, particularly in speeches during
and after his consulship, lends a certain weight and dignity to the
case of his clients, and sometimes even becomes the focal point

of the speech, shifting the emphasis from the actual issue of the case to other considerations. His effective portrayal of his client and others involved in the case, particularly through the skillful employment of stereotypes, comic or otherwise, has been extensively explored, with exceptionally fruitful results.[15]

Oratory, because it deals by its very nature with relationships between individuals or between individuals and their community, is perhaps the most culturally specific of all literary genres. An orator's goal is to persuade his audience, a feat that he cannot generally achieve unless he himself is able to relate intimately to the customs, tastes, fears, and desires of his audience. In his theoretical works, Cicero repeatedly admonishes orators who would be effective to become well acquainted with their own social and political milieu, and to adapt their speeches to the tastes of their community and its common modes of thought.[16] Of course, if it was imperative for orators to keep in close touch with the cultural mores of their audience, it is even more essential for those reading and studying the orations, removed from them by more than two millennia, to understand the culturally specific circumstances that are present or that sometimes even pervade a Ciceronian oration.[17] Despite the fact that Cicero did publish his speeches, we must keep in mind that he was functioning in an oral society, a fact that will have had an impact on the compositional modes that he practiced. The physical environment of the Roman Forum, wherein most of his oratory was delivered, imposed certain requirements on orators of that time, requirements that need to be taken into account when one thinks about the speech and its delivery. Other cultural assumptions—about the persuasive power of character, about prejudices, about personal interactions, about the presuppositions imposed by the Roman legal system— are all important considerations that scholars have explored in recent years. Works by Corbeill on invective, Frier on the profession of the jurisconsult, and Riggsby on the Roman conception of the nature of crime are adduced by Craig as exemplars of this category of Ciceronian scholarship.[18] To those who teach Cicero's

orations on a regular basis, these topics seem perhaps almost
to suggest themselves. But by becoming more conversant with
the most recent scholarly work in such areas, teachers at the
secondary and undergraduate level can both equip themselves
to become more perceptive readers of Ciceronian oratory and also
stand better prepared to introduce into their classrooms a deeper
level of inquiry; while students grapple with grammar and syntax,
they can also grapple with questions whose answers can make
Cicero's speeches come alive in unanticipated ways. To illustrate
this contention, let us briefly examine three of the most commonly
taught Ciceronian speeches in the secondary and/or undergraduate
curriculum, *Pro Archia, In Catilinam I,* and *Pro Caelio,* in accor-
dance with these terms. My hope is to demonstrate how, in each
case, these current trends in Ciceronian scholarship converge in
ways that can prove fruitful and enlightening to those who pay
them heed.

Perhaps the first thing that strikes the reader of Cicero's *Pro
Archia* is the long excursus or digression on the virtues of literature, the poet, and the liberal arts, which constitutes more than
half of the speech. Earlier readers have commented that such a
presentation would not be effective or even acceptable in a modern
court of law;[19] one editor of a school edition has even suggested
that Cicero most likely compressed the technical portion of the
speech for his published version, while considerably expanding
the excursus on literature.[20] After introducing students to the
scholarly question of the spoken versus written versions of the
speeches, one might consider posing questions to them such
as the following: What were Cicero's possible motives for publishing this speech? What do the theories espoused by those
scholars who have written on the publication of the speeches
have to offer in this situation? How would approaching the
speech from the view of persuasive-process criticism affect the
way we look at it? What was Cicero's rhetorical challenge? If
we remove the long digression, does the speech stand as a more
or less effective defense of the poet? And more or less effective

in what context? In other words, would the cultural expectations operative in a Roman court of law preclude—or rather would they foster—such a defense?[21]

It might be worthwhile at this point to say something about the role of digressions in Ciceronian oratory in general, and to apply the same types of questions to other Ciceronian orations that incorporate lengthy digressions. Students could read, for example, sections 41–42 of Asconius on the *Pro Milone* (the Latin is fairly simple), then take a look at the speech itself in English translation in order to see how the so-called *pars extra causam* (71–92)—the argument that Clodius' murder was actually beneficial to the state—functions in this speech.[22] The excursus on the optimates (whom Cicero defines as those "who have acted so as to win by their policy the approval of all the best citizens") in the *Pro Sestio* (96–143) is another long digression that functions in effective ways in that speech. How do these digressions contribute to the overall persuasive force of these orations? How would the persuasiveness of the speeches be altered if these sections were removed? Are these situations comparable to that found in the *Pro Archia*?

Next, consider the ways in which Cicero uses both his client's character and, even more important, his own in the speech. The oration was delivered during the year following Cicero's consulship; might this fact have any relevance to the role that Cicero's own character plays in the oration? How does Cicero go about fashioning or constructing his own character?[23] How is Archias portrayed in the speech? What about other, incidental characters? Archias is a Syrian-born poet who writes in Greek and emblematizes the Greek learning that Cicero champions. How did Roman suspicions of and prejudices toward Greek learning affect Cicero's approach to that topic in the speech? Finally, it is generally accepted that Quintus, Cicero's brother, was presiding over the court on that occasion. What, if any, effect does that have on Cicero's approach?

Cicero published the Catilinarian orations in 60 B.C., nearly three years after their delivery to the Senate and people of Rome.

Reviewing the events in Cicero's life and in the Roman state
during this interval might repay the students' investment with
ample interest. What were the ex-consul's motives for publication
at this time? Robert Cape, in a recent article on Cicero's consular
speeches, makes a convincing case for considering the speeches
that Cicero delivered during his consular year as a discrete corpus
of works aimed at leaving a record of what he said and did during
that year, as well as demonstrating "a high-minded political style
of oratory and a similarly high-minded politician."[24] Some scholars
have assumed that Cicero revised these speeches in order to appease
the new political powers in 60 B.C.; others have argued that Cicero,
sensing the increasing threat to his own career resulting from
his actions as consul, inserted various passages to explain his
point of view, to justify his actions, and to emphasize his wisdom
and good sense—in short, to save his career.[25] For example, when
reading *In Catilinam I,* special attention can be drawn to sections
6, 9, 11, and 22. These are among the sections sometimes cited
by scholars as probable later additions to the published version
of the speech. Can we, in fact, be certain that these were later
additions? What would be the purpose of adding them? Could
they have been in the original spoken oration? That is, does the
oration as it stands represent a plausible, convincing act of persuasion? Why or why not? Could there be other, more overarching
considerations for including such passages in the oration?[26]
What special requirements are imposed on the statesman and
his oratory when he finds himself faced with an emergency in
the state—in other words, what are the demands of so-called
"crisis rhetoric"?[27]

Extraordinarily interesting and accessible work has been
done on the *First Catilinarian,* especially in terms of Cicero's
self-presentation. Batstone, in an important 1994 article, argues
that the purpose of the speech is actually to confirm Cicero's
consular *auctoritas;*[28] as Craig (2002a) perceptively comments,
in this reading, "ethical argument thus becomes the end as well
as the means of persuasion" (522). The study of Cicero's portrayal

of himself in this speech and in the other Catilinarians can be extremely rewarding to students, as can the examination of Cicero's characterization of his nemesis, Catiline. Indeed, the portrait painted here and in the other Catilinarians has much in common with portraits of Cicero's other enemies, in particular Verres, Clodius, and Antony, sketched in other times, in other speeches. Students can gather comparisons by doing selected readings in translation from Cicero's speeches that deal with these enemies.[29]

Turning to the *Pro Caelio,* we find a happy intersection of several of the scholarly questions raised above; indeed, the speech offers wonderful opportunities for introducing many of these approaches into the classroom in fruitful and productive ways. The setting and circumstances of the speech (in the court *de vi*—i.e., the court having jurisdiction over cases involving violence or force—during a festival celebration), the array of charges that not only are connected with historical events but also concern interesting points of Roman law and Roman culture, the arguments embraced by Cicero that depend ultimately on a deep and sophisticated understanding of his audience and their cultural mores, all point to the importance, indeed the necessity, of understanding the cultural and social history of first-century B.C. Rome. The glimpse that the speech offers us into the private lives of elite Roman society, the partying at Baiae, the generational gap between the various members of the Claudius family, the possible connections between Clodius, Clodia, and the circle of Catullus, are all topics worthy of exploration, inherently interesting to students, and readily accessible at various levels of engagement.

The question of the published version of the speech intersects interestingly and informatively with persuasive-process analysis in those passages that always seem to give some pause, even to first-time readers of the speech. My students generally comment on how section 38 (and part of 35) mirrors, or almost "doubles," subsequent sections 48–50. A similar set of "doublets" is found in section 28 and sections 41 and 43. If our students are puzzled

by these apparent repetitions, you can imagine how the crowd
of Ciceronian scholars has fretted over them! R. G. Austin, in
his eighth appendix, "Note on the Composition of the Speech,"[30]
lays out very clearly the major scholarly opinions on these "doublets," a couple of which take the entire portion of sections 39–50
as a later addition by Cicero, placed there in the published
version of the speech to rehabilitate any damage to the orator's
reputation that his so-called "wild oats" defense of Caelius might
inflict. Austin and, later, Craig, following Drexler, reject this interpretation, as they examine the speech in a persuasive-process
mode.[31] Cicero, according to their reading, is caught up in a
"vicious circle." Following their line of criticism, Cicero made a
daring and calculated, perhaps even desperate, move in introducing
the love affair between Clodia and Caelius into the trial, for the
more he emphasizes Clodia's role in the affair, the more he leaves
his own client open to condemnation for his participation in it.
Hence, the more vigorously he assails Clodia, the more intensely
he must justify Caelius and his actions, a situation that inevitably
leads to this series of repetitions. Craig likens Cicero's position
to that of a tightrope walker, and he sees him negotiating this
tightrope throughout sections 30–50, wherein his general defense
of sowing wild oats in sections 39–43 is immediately followed
by Cicero's denial "that Caelius could ever have done any such
thing."[32] Thus, the persuasive-process approach identifies the
rhetorical challenge, examines the tactics and strategies adopted
by the orator to meet the challenge, and assesses how such strategies affect the speech, and ultimately the orator's success in
implementing those tactics.

Most who have taught the *Pro Caelio* are familiar with
Katherine Geffcken's justly admired monograph *Comedy in the*
Pro Caelio, which combines an exploration of political, cultural,
and societal considerations with careful analysis of character
(i.e., in terms of the stereotypes of Roman comedy) to elucidate
the persuasive process of the speech. Geffcken's thesis—that
Cicero in a sense provides through his speech his own theatrical

production for the long-suffering jurors, who because of the trial are forced to miss the activities of the Ludi Megalenses— provides a wealth of opportunities for classroom discussion and activity. Obvious among these, the class may choose to explore an actual Roman comedy of Plautus (or scenes from several of his plays), reading all or part of it in Latin or English translation. A showing of the video *A Funny Thing Happened on the Way to the Forum* can provide the perfect break or interlude in the midst of such a unit. Indeed, scholars have explored other aspects of Cicero's rich and varied use of ethical argumentation, any of which would merit further consideration and contribute further insight into the persuasive process of the speech.[33] Students may find particularly fascinating and worthy of further study the question of the degree to which Cicero's characterization of Clodia in the speech actually corresponds to other evidence (primarily Cicero's own letters!) that we have about her.[34] They may be shocked to discover the possibility that Cicero's portrait is, in fact, largely a literary construct aimed at persuading the jury, and that there was, indeed, another side to the notorious femme fatale whom the orator depicts in defense of his client!

In the preceding pages, I have endeavored to outline a few of the more popular scholarly questions and approaches to Ciceronian oratory, pointing out along the way work by scholars in the field that might be readily accessible to teachers, and in most cases students as well. By introducing these topics in a timely and measured way, we can pique the interest of our students in ways that perhaps the ablative absolute and relative clause of characteristic cannot. At the same time, through an exploration of such topics, we can provide for our students a basis for close linguistic study of the text and for a more expansive view of Roman social and political thought, and a deeper and more solid appreciation for the talents of the ancient orator who, faced with the rhetorical challenge of convincing his audience, relied on his own inborn talent, his knowledge of the art of oratory, and his own great experience to plead his case in a way that would ultimately secure a victory and ensure the safety of his client.

NOTES

1. See, e.g., Kennedy 2002.

2. In Cicero's time, the so-called Atticists stressed the use of pure Latin in a style that was plain and elegant. Lysias and Hyperides were their most highly regarded exemplars, and they criticized Cicero for what they considered to be a swollen, emotional, and bombastic style. See Kennedy 1972, 241–46, and especially Wisse 1995.

3. Craig 2002a, 503–31.

4. Asconius, *Mil.* 42 (ed. Clark): *Manet autem illa quoque excepta eius oratio: scripsit vero hanc quam legimus ita perfecte ut iure prima haberi possit.*

5. Ibid., 41.

6. Dio Cassius, *Hist. Rom.* 40.54.3.

7. See Humbert 1925.

8. Stroh 1975, 31–54.

9. See, e.g., Classen 1985, 2–11; Crawford 1984 and 2002; Riggsby 1995 and 1999, 178–84; Narducci 1997, especially 157–73; Alexander 2000.

10. Riggsby 1999, 184.

11. Craig 2002a, 518.

12. Cf. Leeman 1982; also May 1988, 66–69.

13. Cf., e.g., Zetzel 1994; Riggsby 1997.

14. E.g., Kennedy 1968; May 1981.

15. For a detailed explication of Cicero's conception of ethos (and pathos), see Wisse 1989; for Cicero's use of character as a source for persuasion in his speeches, see May 1988.

16. Cf., e.g., *De oratore* 1. 224–30; 2.131, 159, 306, 337; 3.39, 49, 66.

17. On this point, see May 2002a, 49–70.

18. See Corbeill 1996; Frier 1985; Riggsby 1999.

19. Cf., e.g., Lord Brougham's famous comment in his *Eloquence of the Ancients:* "Cicero's speech for Archias, which is exquisitely composed, but of which not more than one-sixth is to the purpose, could not have been delivered in a British Court of Justice."

20. Kelsey 1897: 47.

21. For an excellent analysis of the persuasive process of the *Pro Archia* and of the digression on literature and the noble arts, see Berry 2004.

22. See above, 73–74. For an analysis of the digression in the *Pro Milone,* see May 1979; cf. also May 1988, especially 28–30, 66–68, 74–77, 83–85, 99–104, 134–37.

23. On this point, see in particular Dugan 2001, and more recently, Dugan 2005, 21–74.

24. Cape 2002.

25. Cf. Kennedy 1972, 176–77; also Nisbet 1964, 60–64.

26. For an insightful analysis of the speech vis-à-vis such questions, see Craig 1993b.

27. Cf. Cape 2002, 143; Kiewe 1994; Wooten 1983.

28. Batstone 1994.

29. For one aspect of this portrayal, see May 1996; see also Habinek 1998.

30. Austin 1960, 159–61.

31. Craig 1995; Drexler 1944.

32. Craig 1995, 413.

33. Cf., e.g., Dorey 1958; Gaffney 1995; Hughes 1997; Leen 2001; Lintott 1967; May 1995; Ramage 1984.

34. On this point, see especially Skinner 1983 and Craig 1995, 417–18.

REFERENCES

Alexander, Michael C. 2000. "The Repudiated Technicality in Roman Forensic Oratory." In Michael Hoeflich, ed., *Lex et Romanitas: Essays for Alan Watson,* 59–72. Berkeley: Robbins Collection Publications, School of Law, University of California.

Austin, Roland G., ed. 1960. *M. Tulli Ciceronis Pro M. Caelio Oratio.* 3rd ed. Oxford: Oxford University Press.

Batstone, William W. 1994. "Cicero's Construction of Consular *Ethos* in the *First Catilinarian.*" *Transactions of the American Philological Association* 124: 211–66.

Berry, D. H. 2004. "Literature and Persuasion in Cicero's *Pro Archia.*" In Jonathan Powell and Jeremy Paterson, eds., *Cicero the Advocate,* 291–311. Oxford: Oxford University Press.

Cape, Jr., Robert W. 2002. "Cicero's Consular Speeches." In James M. May, ed., *Brill's Companion to Cicero: Oratory and Rhetoric,* 113–58. Leiden: E. J. Brill.

Cerutti, Steven. 1993. "James May's *Trials of Character* and Current Trends in the Scholarship on Ciceronian Persuasion." *Classical Bulletin* 69: 83–88.

Classen, Carl J. 1985. *Recht—Rhetorik—Politik.* Darmstadt: Wissenschaftliche Buchgesellschaft.

Corbeill, Anthony. 1996. *Controlling Laughter: Political Humor in the Late Roman Republic.* Princeton, N.J.: Princeton University Press.

Craig, Christopher P. 1993a. *Form as Argument in Cicero's Speeches: A Study of Dilemma.* American Classical Studies, 31. Atlanta: Scholars Press.

———. 1993b. "Three Simple Questions for Teaching Cicero's *First Catilinarian.*" *Classical Journal* 88: 255–67.

———. 1995. "Teaching Cicero's Speech for Caelius: What Enquiring Minds Want to Know." *Classical Journal* 90: 407–22.

———. 2002a. "A Survey of Selected Recent Work on Cicero's *Rhetorica* and Speeches." In James M. May, ed., *Brill's Companion to Cicero: Oratory and Rhetoric,* 503–31. Leiden: E. J. Brill.

———. 2002b. "Bibliography, Including Items on Cicero's Speeches and Rhetorical Works from 1974–1999, with Some Earlier and Later Items, and with All Items Cited in the Chapter Bibliographies in This Volume." In James M. May, ed., *Brill's Companion to Cicero: Oratory and Rhetoric,* 533–99. Leiden: E. J. Brill.

Crawford, Jane W. 1984. *M. Tullius Cicero: The Lost and Unpublished Orations.* Göttingen: Vandenhoeck & Ruprecht.

————. 2002. "The Lost and Fragmentary Orations." In James M. May, ed., *Brill's Companion to Cicero: Oratory and Rhetoric,* 305–30. Leiden: E. J. Brill.

Dorey, T. A. 1958. "Cicero, Clodia, and the *Pro Caelio.*" *Greece & Rome* 5: 175–80.

————, ed. 1964. *Cicero.* London: Routledge & Kegan Paul.

Drexler, H. 1944. "Zu Ciceros Rede *pro Caelio.*" *Nachrichten von der Akademie der Wissenschaften in Göttingen,* Phil.-Hist. Kl.: 1–32.

Dugan, John. 2001. "How to Make (and Break) a Cicero: *Epideixis,* Textuality, and Self-Fashioning in the *Pro Archia* and *In Pisonem.*" *Classical Antiquity* 20: 35–77.

————. 2005. *Making a New Man: Ciceronian Self-Fashioning in the Rhetorical Works.* Oxford: Oxford University Press.

Frier, Bruce. 1985. *The Rise of the Roman Jurists: Studies in Cicero's Pro Caecina.* Princeton, N.J.: Princeton University Press.

Gaffney, G. Edward. 1995. "*Severitati respondere:* Character Drawing in *Pro Caelio* and in Catullus' *Carmina.*" *Classical Journal* 90: 423–31.

Geffcken, Katherine. 1973. *Comedy in the* Pro Caelio *(with an appendix on the* In Clodium et Curionem*).* Leiden: Brill.

Habinek, Thomas N. 1998. "Cicero and the Bandits." In Habinek, *The Politics of Latin Literature: Writing, Identity, and Empire in Ancient Rome,* 69–87. Princeton, N.J.: Princeton University Press.

Hughes, Joseph J. 1997. "*Inter tribunal et scaenam:* Comedy and Rhetoric at Rome." In William J. Dominik, ed., *Roman Eloquence: Rhetoric in Society and Literature,* 182–97. London and New York: Routledge.

Humbert, Jules. 1925. *Les plaidoyers écrits et les plaidoiries réelles de Cicéron.* Paris: Presses Universitaires de France.

Kelsey, Francis W. 1897. *Select Orations and Letters of Cicero.* Boston: Allyn and Bacon.

Kennedy, George A. 1968. "The Rhetoric of Advocacy in Greece and Rome." *American Journal of Philology* 89: 419–36.

————. 1972. *The Art of Rhetoric in the Roman World.* Princeton, N.J.: Princeton University Press.

————. 2002. "Cicero's Oratorical and Rhetorical Legacy." In James M. May, ed., *Brill's Companion to Cicero: Oratory and Rhetoric,* 481–502. Leiden: E. J. Brill.

Kiewe, Amos. 1994. *The Modern Presidency and Crisis Rhetoric.* Westport, Conn.: Praeger.

Leeman, A. D. 1982. "The Technique of Persuasion in Cicero's *Pro Murena.*" In Walther Ludwig, ed., *Éloquence et Rhétorique chez Cicéron,* 193–228. Entretiens sur l'Antiquité Classique, 28. Geneva: Fondation Hardt.

Leen, Anne. 2001. "*Clodia Oppugnatrix:* The *Domus* Motif in Cicero's *Pro Caelio.*" *Classical Journal* 96: 141–64.

Lintott, A. W. 1967. "P. Clodius—Felix Catilina?" *Greece & Rome* 14: 157–69.

May, James M. 1979. "The *Ethica Digressio* and Cicero's *Pro Milone:* A Progression of Intensity from *Logos* to *Ethos* to *Pathos.*" *Classical Journal* 74: 240–46.

————. 1981. "The Rhetoric of Advocacy and Patron-Client Identification: Variation on a Theme." *American Journal of Philology* 102: 308–15.

————. 1988. *Trials of Character: The Eloquence of Ciceronian Ethos.* Chapel Hill and London: University of North Carolina Press.

————. 1995. "Patron and Client, Father and Son in Cicero's *Pro Caelio.*" *Classical Journal* 90: 433–41.

————. 1996. "Cicero and the Beasts." *Syllecta Classica* 7: 143–53.

————. 2002a. "Ciceronian Oratory in Context." In James M. May, ed., *Brill's Companion to Cicero: Oratory and Rhetoric,* 49–70. Leiden: E. J. Brill.

————, ed. 2002b. *Brill's Companion to Cicero: Oratory and Rhetoric.* Leiden: E. J. Brill.

Narducci, Emanuele. 1997. *Cicerone e l'eloquenza Romana: Retorica e progetto culturale.* Rome: Laterza.

Neumeister, Christoff. 1964. *Grundsätze der forensischen Rhetorik gezeigt an Gerichtsreden Ciceros.* Langue et parole, Sprach- und Literaturstrukturelle Studien, 3. Munich: M. Hüber.

Nisbet, R. G. M. 1964. "The Speeches." In Thomas A. Dorey, ed., *Cicero,* 47–79. London: Routledge & Kegan Paul.

Ramage, Edwin S. 1984. "Clodia in Cicero's *Pro Caelio*." In David F. Bright and Edwin S. Ramage, eds., *Classical Texts and Their Tradition: Studies in Honor of C.R. Trahman*, 201–11. Chico, Calif.: Scholars Press.

Riggsby, Andrew M. 1995. "Pliny on Cicero and Oratory: Self-Fashioning in the Public Eye." *American Journal of Philology* 116: 123–35.

———. 1997. "Did the Romans Believe in Their Verdicts?" *Rhetorica* 15: 235–51.

———. 1999. *Crime and Community in Ciceronian Rome*. Austin: University of Texas Press.

Skinner, Marilyn B. 1983. "Clodia Metelli." *Transactions of the American Philological Association* 113: 273–87.

Stroh, Wilfried. 1975. *Taxis und Taktik*. Stuttgart: Teubner.

Vasaly, Ann. 1993. *Representations: Images of the World in Ciceronian Oratory*. Berkeley, Los Angeles, and Oxford: University of California Press.

Wisse, Jakob. 1989. *Ethos and Pathos from Aristotle to Cicero*. Amsterdam: Hakkert.

———. 1995. "Greeks, Romans, and the Rise of Atticism." In J. G. J. Abbenes, S. R. Slings, and I. Sluiter, eds., *Greek Literary Theory after Aristotle: A Collection of Papers in Honor of D.M. Schenkeveld*, 65–82. Amsterdam: VU University Press.

Wooten, Cecil W. 1983. *Cicero's Philippics and Their Demosthenic Model*. Chapel Hill: University of North Carolina Press.

Zetzel, James E. G. 1994. Review of C. P. Craig, *Form as Argument in Cicero's Speeches*. Atlanta: Scholars Press, 1993. *Bryn Mawr Classical Review* 94.1.5.

CHAPTER 5

DIDO IN TRANSLATION

Richard F. Thomas

The purpose of the following discussion of the Dido episode
from the *Aeneid* is to map out some ways in which reception
study can be used to engage students in reflection on central
aspects of the *Aeneid*.[1] By "reception study," I mean something
that is not particularly specialized or theoretical, but that is always
closely engaged with texts, namely a highly skeptical and frequently deconstructive way of reading those who have reacted
to the texts of classical antiquity. In this approach, previous
readings are deliberately destabilized and shown as subject to
the ideological, religious, or ethical peculiarities to which all
reading communities (our own included) are prone. This sort of
study implies a close and constant relationship with the original
source texts as with the receiving texts. By engaging the latter,
students can move outside the usual constraints that come from
studying the source text in isolation from the traditions that it
generates. In the adaptations, translations, and commentaries on
Virgil, we find discourse about precisely the issues that most attract
the attention of the contemporary student. Chief among such
issues are ideological questions that arise from the poem's exploration of the characters who stand in the way of Aeneas' mission
to found Rome, in particular Dido and Turnus.[2] This essay will

treat Dido particularly through the lens of translation, which is just one form of reception, but one that is notable in that the translator is compelled to confront every word of the source text. Omissions, distortions, and other subjectivities become more easily apparent than in other forms of interpretive activity, with the result that the translation may function as an indicator of problematic passages in the original.

To those of us who have spent many years with the *Aeneid,* the judgment of Aeneas' actions with regard to Dido, the role of the gods in inflicting on her an emotional condition that will lead to her doom, the extent to which she is culpable, these may be very old chestnuts. But for the student encountering this story for the first time, such questions are still vibrant, and it is always a challenge for us to match our students' eager engagement with Dido and Aeneas. By having recourse to reception studies, the instructor can demonstrate that such matters are indeed timeless, even while they may have become very familiar to us as teachers. Students can also observe the way different ages, and differing moral perspectives, can produce variety in readings; and so they may situate themselves in communities of readers, going literally right back to the time of composition of the poem. For instance, the contemporary "oppositional" reader who has a more critical stance toward the actions of Aeneas in *Aen.* 4 may identify with Chaucer, who himself works in a tradition that goes back to Ovid's sympathetic Dido treatment in *Heroides* 7. This poem is of great interest in its own right, and is also very useful in beginning discussion of the Dido reception. Ovid's decision to present the conflict through the exclusive eyes of Dido, unmediated by any narrative frame, obviously stacks the deck against the figure of Aeneas. As a result, many of the ambiguities about blame, responsibility, and causation are removed, with the possibility of a clear-cut criticism of the actions of the "hero." The Chaucerian voice, a development of the Ovidian, expresses clear sympathy and clear criticism of the Augustan point of view:

And after grave was, how shee
Made of him, shortly, at oo word,
Hir lyf, hir love, hir luste, hir lord;
And dide him al the reverence,
And leyde on him al the dispence,
That any woman mighte do,
Weninge hit had al be so,
As he hir swoor; and her-by demed
That he was good, for he swich semed.
Allas! what harm doth apparence,
Whan hit is fals in existence!
For he to hir a traitour was;
Wherfor she slow hir-self, allas![3]

Whether or not the Virgilian narrative point of view endorses
the Ovidian—or, for that matter, the Virgilian—Dido's accusa-
tion against Aeneas (*Aen.* 4.305–30, 365–87; *Heroides* 7.67–68,
195–96) is a matter open to interpretation, but one closed off by
Chaucer, who plainly states that Aeneas was indeed a traitor.
Here we have not translation per se, but reception that finds its
impetus in translating and transferring.

I have found it particularly useful to evaluate the ethical
issues to which the Dido story gives rise through translation,
including the students' translation. A student who confronts the
task of translating *Aen.* 4.165–72 will have to deal with words
such as *pronuba* (Juno's status looks formal), *conubiis/coniu-
gium* (what is the difference?), and *culpam* ("fault," "flaw," or
"slip"?). The act of translating can thus lay bare the hermeneutic
enterprise of the translator, a useful pedagogic move. No translation of the *Aeneid* is more revealing of moral prejudice, or
more influential in a general way, than the version of John
Dryden (1697), who makes his views clear in his notes on the
Lavinia episode from Book 12:

But I am much deceived, if . . . there be not a secret
satire against the [female] sex, which is lurking under

this description of Virgil, who seldom speaks well of women . . . The rest [besides Camilla, Andromache, and Venus—"a better mother than a wife"] are Junos, Dianas, Didos, Amatas, two mad prophetesses, three Harpies on earth, and as many Furies under ground. This fable of Lavinia includes a secret moral; that women, in their choice of husbands, prefer the younger of their suitors to the elder; are insensible of merit, fond of handsomeness, and, generally speaking, rather hurried away by their appetite, than governed by their reason.[4]

These words reflect Dryden's apparent misogyny, and they also reflect the fact that he openly speaks, in the preface to his translation, of the perfection of the character of Aeneas, whom he presents as the ideal monarch. Teachers may test the legitimacy of Dryden's assessment of Lavinia, and of all the female players of the poem, and so bring a broader, and likely more skeptical, point of view to Dryden's depiction of Dido herself.

So much for the ideological perspective; now for the aesthetic. In a well-known passage of the *Examen Poeticum* (1693), John Dryden defends his preference for "paraphrase, or translation with latitude," which occupies a middle ground between the more literal "metaphrase," on the one hand, and free "imitation,"' on the other.[5] Moreover, in his *Life of Lucian,* Dryden says:

A translator that would write with any force or spirit of an original must never dwell on the words of his author. He ought to possess himself entirely and *perfectly comprehend the genius of his author,* the nature of the subject, and the terms of the art or subject treated of. And then he will express himself as justly, and with as much life, as if he wrote an original; whereas he who copies word for word loses all spirit in the tedious transfusion . . . [emphasis added][6]

True as that may be, and is, of the aesthetic reception of the translator's work, it immediately points to problematic aspects of translation as interpretation, for "perfect comprehension," particularly of the ideological aspects of poetry, will always be elusive, rooted in subjectivity, and in high likelihood contestable. The potential for a particularly insidious form of circularity is great. And in the "Dedication of the *Aeneis*," Dryden is quite clear about his procedure: "Some things too I have omitted, and sometimes have added of my own. Yet the omissions I hope, are but of Circumstances, and such as would have no grace in *English;* and the Additions, I also hope, are easily deduc'd from Virgil's Sense."[7] We shall soon observe some of those additions.

With this theoretical background, there is little surprise, then, that we find Dryden intervening in violent ways in his translation of pivotal Dido passages, where we find a strong, poetically appealing, and therefore rhetorically convincing confluence of his apparent misogyny (*Aeneid* as secret satire on women) with his assumptions about Virgilian misogyny (perfect comprehension of his author). Dido is inflamed by the combined effects of Cupid/Ascanius' implanting erotic desire, Aeneas' heroic tales, and Anna's persuasive seductive words to her sister (line numbers according to Virgil, *Aeneid,* and Dryden's *Aeneis*).

uritur infelix Dido totaque vagatur urbe furens   4.68–69

Sick with desire, *and seeking him she loves,*
From Street to Street, the raving Dido roves
        [emphasis added]   4.93–94

obstipuit primo aspectu Sidonia Dido,
casu deinde viri tanto, et sic ore locuta est.   1.613–14

The Tyrian Queen stood fix'd upon his Face,
Pleas'd with his Motions, ravish'd with his Grace;

Admir'd his Fortunes, *more admir'd the Man;*
Then recollected stood; and thus began . . .   1.866–69

In each instance the translator has added an emphasis not present
in Virgil's Latin, and in each instance the result is a strong version,
which takes the reader to a point well beyond that of the original. This is striking particularly in the lines from Book 1, which
precede the erotic infection of Dido by Cupid/Ascanius.
Dryden's Dido, "fix'd upon his Face," needs no input from such
machines; in Dryden's rewriting, it is a flaw of character that will
be her downfall.

So much for Dido's first encounter with Aeneas; her last, in
the Underworld, is also revealing in Dryden's version, commu-
nicating a strong sense of misogyny by interpolations and other
means. The catalogue of tragic lovers in the Campi Lugentes
(Plains of Grief) gives some examples. Pasiphae and Phaedra,
not together in Virgil, are united and then characterized in
Dryden's translation:

He saw Pasiphae there/ With Phaedra's ghost,
    a foul incestuous pair   6.604–605

The italicized detail, rendered emphatic by the final rhymed
position in the couplet, finds no analogue in the *Aeneid.* On the
contrary, the Virgilian reality is far different: at *Aen.* 6.442–44,
the poet is markedly sympathetic to the condition of these literary heroines:

hic quos durus amor crudeli tabe peredit
secreti celant calles et myrtea circum
silva tegit; curae non ipsa in morte relinquunt

Here those whom harsh love has consumed with cruel wasting are
hidden by remote paths and hemmed in by myrtle woods; not
even in death do their cares leave them [my translation]

Dryden, on the other hand, exults in their fate:

> The Souls, whom that unhappy Flame invades,
> In secret solitude, and Myrtle shades,
> *Make endless Moans, and pining with Desire*
> *Lament too late their unextinguish'd Fire.*   6.598–601

I have suggested that Dryden's introduction of wailing and other noises emitted by these women (they are completely silent in Virgil's account) may show a debt to Dante, who more emphatically consigned them to a Christian Hell (*Inferno* 5.25–39):

> Ora incomincian le *dolente note*   25
>   *a farmisi sentire;* or son venuto
>   là dove *molto pianto mi percuote.*
> Io venni in luogo d'ogni luce muto,
>   che *mugghia come fa mar per tempesta,*
>   se da contrari venti è combattuto.   30
> La bufera infernal, che mai non resta,
>   mena la spirti con la sua rapina:
>   voltando e percotendo li molesta.
> Quando giugnon davanti alla ruina,
>   quivi *le strida, il compianto, il lamento;*   35
>   bestemmian quivi la virtù divina.
> Intesi ch' a così fatto tormento
>   enno dannati i peccator carnali,
>   che la ragion sommettono al talento.

Now the *doleful strains* began to attract my attention; now am I come to where *much wailing struck me.* I came into the place mute of all light which was *bellowing as the sea does* in a storm when buffeted by opposing winds. The infernal storm which never rests snatches up and drives the spirits: spinning and striking them it brings them torment. When they come before its downrush, *there are shriekings, weepings and lamentations;* they *blaspheme* there the power of God. And I learned that carnal sinners who subject reason to desire are to such torments damned.

Whether or not Dryden drew from Dante, both seem eager to provide a moralizing commentary on a Virgilian passage that is utterly open on the question of blame and responsibility.

The general enterprise, for Dryden and for other translators, was to protect the heroism of Aeneas, to put the blame on Dido alone, as, for instance, when the translator familiarizes the exotic purple cloak in which Dido decks Aeneas out: *Aen.* 4.162–63, *Tyrioque ardebat murice laena demissa ex umeris* "and a cloak of Tyrian purple hung gleaming from his shoulders." Such dress is a sign of Eastern luxury, and a Roman reader would have been shocked to find Rome's ultimate founder so dressed. But Dryden can take care of such shock; his version makes the detail mundane:

> A purple Scarf, with Gold embroider'd o'er,
> (Queen *Dido*'s Gift) about his Waste he wore.

What was exotic, Eastern, effeminate, very troubling in its Roman context for a Roman reader, is thus transformed into the familiar, English, and militarily correct, as is clear from the following:

> Lost: An officer's scarf with four gold Fringes around
> the Waist, set on Crimson Silk, and a very deep Fringe
> at each end.[8]

There can be no doubt about the reaction of a reader of the target text (in this case Dryden, as distinct from the source language, Virgil). Dryden's contemporary reader would have had a neutral reaction to Aeneas' scarf: that is what an officer and a gentleman would have worn in 1697. So we can see the late-seventeenth-century reader of Dryden's "translation" being manipulated into an ideologically positive assessment of Aeneas at this most disturbing (from the Virgilian perspective) moment.

Syntax can just as easily be changed to produce the right outcome, as at 4.189–94, where rumors of Aeneas' and Dido's dalliances are related:

haec tum multiplici populos sermone replebat
gaudens, et pariter facta atque infecta canebat: 190
venisse Aenean Troiano sanguine cretum,
cui se pulchra viro dignetur iungere Dido;
nunc hiemem inter se luxu, quam longa, *fovere*
regnorum *immemores* turpique cupidine *captos.*

The plurals *immemores* and *captos* make it quite clear that
Dido and Aeneas are both the subject of *fovere:* Rumor reports
that Dido and Aeneas are spending the winter in intimate luxury, both forgetful of their regal duties. Dryden will have none
of that:

She fills the Peoples Ears with *Dido*'s Name;
Who, lost to Honour, and the Sense of Shame,
Admits into her Throne and Nuptial Bed
A wandering Guest, who from his Country fled:
Whole days with him *she passes in delights;*
And wastes in Luxury long Winter nights:
Forgetful of her Fame and Royal Trust;
Dissolv'd in Ease, abandon'd to her Lust.

The reader who substitutes these verses for the Virgilian original
will form a very different opinion of Dido and of Aeneas—as
Dryden intended.

I also find it useful to have students compare multiple translations, particularly when the lines in question are subject to
differing ideological interpretations, as happens at *Aen.* 4.283–84.
Mercury has visited Aeneas and communicated Jupiter's will to
him; he must sail for Italy. These verses capture the moment at
which Aeneas accepts that he must leave Dido, but ponders how
to do so safely:

heu quid agat? quo nunc reginam ambire furentem
audeat adfatu? quae prima exordia sumat?

Ah, what to do? With what sort of address is he to dare get
around the queen in her rage? What opening preface to
adopt? [my trans.]

The following versions represent a selection from the nineteenth
and twentieth centuries, and in each case students may be shown
how these readers struggle to justify the traditional view of
Aeneas' heroism with the fact that in the Latin (*ambire*) there is
a hint of deception. From its root sense of "go around," it early
acquired the sense of "solicit," "canvass," but also "get around"
and even "entrap," as at *Aen.* 7.333, where Juno accuses Aeneas
and his men of "entrapping Latinus with a marriage proposal"
(*conubiis ambire Latinum*).[9]

Bowen:	Whither, alas! shall he turn? How *face* the infuriate Queen?
	How may he dare to approach her? the tale how break to her ear?
Conington:	He yearns to leave the dear, dear land.
	But how to fly? or how *accost*
	The queen, by eddying passion tost?
	How charm the ravings of distress?
	What choice to make when hundreds press?
Fairfax Taylor:	Ah! what to do? what opening can he find
	To break the news, the infuriate queen *withstand*?
Davidson:	Ah! what can he do? in what terms can he now presume to *solicit the consent of* the raving queen?
Lonsdale/Lee:	Alas what is he to do? with what address can he now dare to try *to conciliate* the frantic queen? what opening can he adopt?
Cranch:	And yet alas!
	What shall he do? With what speech shall he now Dare to *appease* the raging queen? How first Begin to speak?

Morris: Ah, what to do? and with what word may he be bold
                   to *win*
                   Peace of the Queen all mad with love? What wise
                   shall he begin?

Rickards: But how approach the queen? how frame the words
                   Of parting, and her fierce resentment *brave*?

Richardson: But O what could he do? How *meet the scene,*
                   And *brave the passion of* the raging queen?

Richards: What can he do, how *coax* the frenzied queen
                   Or dare address her, what first opening choose?

Jackson Knight: But what could he do? How could he dare to speak
                   to the infatuated queen, and *win her round*? What
                   would be the best opening for him to choose?

Salt: What shall he do? How *bring* the infatuate queen
                   Those tidings? How make preface to such tale?

And then there is Dryden:

Dryden: What should he say? Or how should he begin?
                   What course, alas! remains, to steer between
                   Th' offended lover and the pow'rful queen?

In many ways, Dryden remains truer to the Latin than do
many of his nineteenth-century followers, perhaps because, as I
have suggested, he was unconcerned by Aeneas' actions, which
were perfectly acceptable when held up to the standard of mid-
to late-seventeenth-century courtly attitudes toward divorce and
abandonment. Dryden in his introduction expressed his debt to
the French royalist critic Jean Regnault de Segrais, whose translation of Virgil, "avec privilege du roi," was published in two
volumes in the years before Dryden began his own, but more
importantly in the years in which Dryden held a central place in
the English court (Paris 1668, 1681). Segrais, in fact, like Dryden

in his "Dedication," responds to those who think that Virgil in any
way vitiated the perfection of his hero, perhaps most strikingly
when he states (reasonably) that we should not judge the ancients
by the standards of other eras. His example? No need to be concerned about Aeneas' treatment of Dido, since Segrais projects
onto Augustan Rome the tolerance for abandonment and divorce
that we find in the French and English courts of the late seven-
teenth century: "Le divorce passoit à Rome pour une galanterie;
& l'Empereur auquel il vouloit plaire, l'avait autorisé dans sa
famille" ("In Rome divorce passed as a gallantry, and the
emperor whom Virgil would want to please had authorized it in
his own family").[10] Charles II, in whose reign Dryden flourished,
would certainly have gone along with this, although he did not
bother with divorce. And so this "courtly" attitude toward divorce
makes Dryden, paradoxically, one of the most honest of translators of some parts of *Aen.* 4. Aeneas' actions did not disturb
him; no need therefore to change Virgil.

In spite of all this, a few lines later in *Aen.* 4, when the
Virgilian Aeneas seems to be urging his men to dissimulate,
even Dryden becomes uneasy, and makes one of his famous
interpolations:

> sese interea, quando optima Dido
> nesciat et tantos rumpi non speret amores,
> temptaturum aditus et quae mollissima fandi
> tempora, quis rebus dexter modus. ocius omnes
> imperio laeti parent et iussa facessunt.   4.291–95

> Himself, meantime, the softest hours would choose,
> Before the love-sick lady heard the news,
> And move her tender mind, by slow degrees
> *To suffer what the sovereign power decrees:*
> *Jove will inspire him when and what to say.*
> They hear with pleasure and with haste obey.

The italicized lines find no equivalent in the Latin, but they well serve the function of assigning to Jupiter the responsibility for Aeneas' deceptive plans for leaving Carthage.

In *Virgil and the Augustan Reception*, I suggested that one nineteenth-century translator, John Davis Long, something of an amateur Virgilian, was able to see the flawed heroism of Aeneas, particularly with regard to his treatment of Dido.[11] John Davis Long is to my mind and for any classicist a remarkable figure.[12] Secretary of the Navy under William McKinley, this Harvard graduate, Boston lawyer, and translator of the *Aeneid* might well have become president of the United States had Theodore Roosevelt not behaved so flamboyantly in the Spanish-American War, and so put himself in the limelight before the 1900 Republican convention, at which he became the vice-presidential nominee. Twenty years before the sinking of the *Maine* in Havana harbor, Long, having just been elected speaker of the Massachusetts House of Representatives for the third time, noted in his journal (January 17, 1878), "A quiet day. Buy Bryant's *Iliad* and *Odyssey*. Read a book in the former." Five days later (January 22), presumably as a result of this activity, he records, "Begin this evening a translation of Virgil. Perhaps I shall finish it and publish." For the next year, we find steady references to his task, which enters into the rhythms of his family life, his activities in his law practice, and the workings of the state legislature. It was Long's memory of Virgil and his boyhood love of Virgil and Latin poetry that brought him back to the poet. One of his earliest entries in the journal comes from Monday, July 24, 1848; the nine-year-old boy writes excitedly:

A cloudy, rainy, misty, and muddy day. Our school keeps two or three weeks longer. *I have begun the study of Latin* [Long's emphasis]. Zadoc [his brother] will hear me recite.

And in the preface to the *Aeneid* translation, he harks back to those days:

> Perhaps some will read this. If so, they will renew, as I after twenty-five years have done, not only the kindly acquaintance of this Roman story-teller, but the happy morning of the school-boy's shining face and eager heart.

This by way of background, then, on John Davis Long the man; here is his response as a translator to *Aen.* 4.283–84:

> Alas for him!
> What can he do? with what excuse now dare
> To cheat the queen whose love to madness grows?
> What step the first to take?

Long elsewhere may be usefully juxtaposed with Dryden, with whom he makes a telling contrast, as, for instance, in the poignant passage at 4.522–33:

> nox erat et placidum carpebant fessa soporem
> corpora per terras, silvaeque et saeva quierant
> aequora, cum medio volvuntur sidera lapsu,
> cum tacet omnis ager, pecudes pictaeque volucres,   525
> quaeque lacus late liquidos quaeque aspera dumis
> rura tenent, somno positae sub nocte silenti.   527
> at non infelix animi Phoenissa, neque umquam   529
> solvitur in somnos oculisve aut pectore noctem   530
> accipit: ingeminant curae rursusque resurgens
> saevit amor magnoque irarum fluctuat aestu.
> sic adeo insistit secumque ita corde volutat

The poetry of Long's version is of a high order, and it is perhaps unsurprising that this father of two daughters and early supporter of women's suffrage responded with particular empathy to these lines. Indeed, Long's lines may be even more empathetic than

Virgil's original, particularly toward the end of the passage. I
juxtapose his version with the closing lines of that of Dryden,
who lacks empathy perhaps to a comparable degree to which
Long adds it:

> 'Twas night; and weariness o'er all the earth
> In peaceful slumber sank to rest. No breath
> Was in the woods or on the fitful sea.
> It was the time when, half their circuit o'er,
> The stars began to fall; when fields and flocks
> Lay still, and birds were nestling 'neath their wings
> Of many hues; when all that lives within
> The water depths, and all that in the fields
> And forest dwell, under the silent night
> In deep sleep lying, dreamed all care away,
> And human hearts forgot that life is toil.
> But not the aching heart of Dido. Ne'er
> In slumber resteth she, nor in her breast
> Nor on her eyes the blessing of the night.
> Her soul is dark; her love springs fresh again,
> And wild with every gust of passion beats.
> So now she ponders and her heart o'erflows . . . (Long)

> All else of Nature's common gift partake;
> Unhappy Dido was alone awake.
> Nor sleep nor ease the furious queen can find:
> Sleep fled her eyes as quiet fled her mind.
> Despair and rage and love, divide her heart;
> Despair and rage had some, but love the greater part.
> Then thus she said within her secret mind . . . (Dryden 4.767–73)

I will conclude with the famous cave scene, often a site for heated
discussion and debate among students, as among scholars (4.165–72):

> speluncam Dido dux et Troianus eandem   165
> deveniunt. prima et Tellus et pronuba Iuno

dant signum; fulsere ignes et conscius aether
conubiis summoque ulularunt vertice Nymphae.
ille dies primus leti primusque malorum
causa fuit; neque enim specie famaue movetur   170
nec iam furtivum Dido meditatur amorem:
coniugium vocat, hoc praetexit nomine culpam.

Is it a wedding, as Dido believes and Aeneas will deny, or not?
A divine but not an earthly union? What to make of the divine
authority in that the encounter is based on the scheming of Venus
and Juno—with Jupiter out of the picture? The narrator calls it
conubia; Dido, *coniugium.* What is the difference? Who led whom?
Is *dux* doing double duty? What and how bad is a *culpa* in such a
situation? Our two translators show different ways of proceeding:

> But Dido and the Trojan chief
> Seek the same cave. Primeval goddess Earth
> And Juno, goddess of wooing, give
> The signal. Lightnings flash, the very air
> Glows conscious with this wedlock, and the nymphs
> Flit shrieking on the mountain top. That day
> The seed of death and woes to come was sown.
> It matters not to Dido what is said,
> Or what the look, for now no more she thinks
> Of blushing for her love, but says his wife
> She is, and hides her slip beneath that name. (Long)

> The queen and prince, as love or fortune guides,
> One common cavern in her bosom hides,
> Then first the trembling earth the signal gave;
> And flashing fires enlighten all the cave:
> Hell from below, and Juno from above,
> And howling nymphs, were conscious to their love.
> From this ill-omened hour, in time arose,
> Debate and death, and all succeeding woes.
> The queen, whom sense of honour could not move,

No longer made a secret of her love,
But called it marriage; by that specious name
To veil the crime, and sanctify the shame. (Dryden)

Again Long empathizes, and is more honest with the Virgilian text: *pronuba Iuno* is "Juno, goddess of wooing," *conubiis* is "wedlock, " *culpam* is "slip," and so on. Dryden rewrites and interpolates: gone is *pronuba, conubiis* is "love" (i.e., "sex"), "Hell" is a witness to the union, and *culpam* has become a "crime," embedded in a closing couplet that is totally free from moral relativism: Dido is a criminal, and so deserves whatever will come her way. With passages such as these, the choice of how we read remains open to us, and the fact that a translator closes off such choice merely underscores the openness of the Virgilian text—as long as we keep going back to it. Thus the study of translation can amount to a study of interpretive reception, and students can be encouraged to recognize in competing translations competing interpretations that are still very much a part of the scholarly landscape. They can then return to the Latin of Virgil and observe the manipulations and prejudices of the translator, with all that this implies in the contestation of reading.

NOTES

1. Much of this article is developed directly from "Dido and Her Translators," chap. 5 of Thomas 2001. It appears with permission from Cambridge University Press.

2. It is probably right to say that there is no great consensus in the ideological reading of the *Aeneid*. What I call the "Augustan reading" (Thomas 2001, xii–xx) may best be represented in Cairns 1989 and Hardie 1986, while Lyne 1987, O'Hara 1990, and Thomas 2001 are exemplary of "oppositional readings." Hardie 1993 suggests that there has in recent years been more of a drift from the former position toward the latter than in the opposite direction.

3. Chaucer, *The Hous of Fame* 1: 256–68. The poem of Chaucer (ca. 1342–1400) reflects the generally Ovidian point of view that is to be found throughout the Middle Ages in the vernacular Dido romance tradition; see Thomas 2001, 154–59.

4. Dryden 1909, 12.100–102. We are particularly well served by the fact that Dryden's translation of the *Aeneid* is accompanied by an extensive dedication and introduction, and followed by detailed "Notes and Observations."

5. Kinsley 1961, viii. "Sure I am, that if it be a fault, 'tis much more pardonable, than that of those, who run into the other extream, of a literal, and close Translation, where the Poet is constrained so streightly to his Author's Words, that he wants elbow-room, to express his Elegancies. He leaves him obscure; he leaves him Prose, where he found him Verse."

6. Thus Dryden in Watson 1962; included in Schulte and Biguenet 1992, 29–31.

7. Frost and Dearing 1987, 5.329.

8. *OED,* 1689 entry from the *London Gazette.*

9. See Horsfall 2000. See Clausen 2002, 84–85, for discussion of *ambire* at 4.283, including reference to T. E. Page's view that "it hints at cunning and treachery," and Servius Danielis' *blanditiis vel subdole circumvenire,* "to circumvent by flattery or guile." Clausen prefers Austin's "to canvass."

10. Thomas 2001, 140.

11. Ibid., 173–89.

12. For a fuller account, see Thomas 1995.

References

Bowen, Charles, trans. 1887. *Virgil in English Verse:* Eclogues *and* Aeneid *I–VI.* London: Murray.

Cairns, Francis. 1989. *Virgil's Augustan Epic.* Cambridge: Cambridge University Press.

Clausen, Wendell. 2002. *Virgil's* Aeneid: *Decorum, Allusion, and Ideology.* Munich and Leipzig: K. G. Saur.

Conington, John, trans. 1865. *P. Vergili Maronis opera: The Works of Virgil.* 2nd ed., rev. and corr. London: Whittaker.

Cranch, Christopher Pearse, trans. 1872. *The Æneid of Virgil.* Boston: J. R. Osgood, 1872.

Davidson, Joseph, trans. 1854. *The Works of Virgil: Literally Translated into English Prose, with Notes.* New ed., revised, with additional notes, by Theodore Alois Buckley. London: Henry G. Bohn.

Dryden, John, trans. 1909. *Æneid.* The Harvard Classics, vol. 13. New York: P. F. Collier & Son.

Frost, William, and Vinton A. Dearing. 1987. *The Works of John Dryden.* Vols. 5–6: *The Works of Virgil in English.* Berkeley, Los Angeles, and London: University of California Press.

Hardie, Philip R. 1986. *Virgil's* Aeneid: *Cosmos and Imperium.* Oxford: Clarendon Press.

———. 1993. *The Epic Successors of Virgil: A Study in the Dynamics of a Tradition.* Cambridge: Cambridge University Press.

Horsfall, Nicholas. 2000. *Vergil,* Aeneid *7: A Commentary.* Leiden, Boston, and Cologne: Brill.

Kinsley, James. 1961. *The Works of Virgil.* Trans. John Dryden. Oxford: Oxford University Press.

Knight, W. F. Jackson, trans. 1956. *The* Aeneid. Baltimore, Md.: Penguin.

Lonsdale, James, and Samuel Lee, trans. 1883. *The Works of Virgil Rendered into English Prose.* London: Macmillan.

Long, John Davis. 1879. *The* Aeneid *of Virgil.* Boston: Joseph Knight.

Lyne, R. O. A. M. 1987. *Further Voices in Vergil's* Aeneid. Oxford: Clarendon Press.

Morris, William, trans. 1876. *The Æneids of Virgil.* Boston: Roberts Brothers.

O'Hara, James J. 1990. *Death and the Optimistic Prophecy in Vergil's* Aeneid. Princeton, N.J.: Princeton University Press.

Richards, Frank, trans. 1931. *The* Aeneid *of Virgil.* Cheap ed. London: J. Murray.

Richardson, E., trans. 1883. *The First Six Books of Vergil's* Aeneid. Woonsocket [R.I.]: Patriot Printing House.

Rickards, G. K., trans. 1871. *The Æneid of Virgil, Books I–VI.* Edinburgh and London: W. Blackwood and Sons.

Salt, Henry S., trans. 1928. *The Story of Æneas: Virgil's* Æneid. Cambridge: Cambridge University Press.

Schulte, Rainer, and John Biguenet. 1992. *Theories of Translation: An Anthology of Essays from Dryden to Derrida.* Chicago and London: University of Chicago Press.

Taylor, E. Fairfax, trans. 1903. *The Twelve Books of Virgil's* Aeneid. London: J. M. Dent.

Thomas, Richard F. 1995. "Browsing in the Western Stacks." *Harvard Library Bulletin* 6.3: 27–33.

———. 2001. *Virgil and the Augustan Reception.* Cambridge: Cambridge University Press.

Watson, George, ed. 1962. *John Dryden: Of Dramatic Poesy and Other Critical Essays.* 2 vols. London: J. M. Dent.

CONTRIBUTORS

Ronnie Ancona is Professor of Classics at Hunter College and The Graduate Center, City University of New York. She is the author of *Time and the Erotic in Horace's Odes* (1994), *Writing Passion: A Catullus Reader* (2004), *Horace: Selected Odes and Satire 1.9* (1999, 2005), and coeditor of *Gendered Dynamics in Latin Love Poetry* (2005).

Barbara Weiden Boyd is the Henry Winkley Professor of Latin and Greek at Bowdoin College, Brunswick, Maine. She is the author of *Ovid's Literary Loves: Influence and Innovation in the Amores* (1997), *Vergil's "Aeneid": Selections from Books 1, 2, 4, 6, 10, and 12* (2nd ed. 2004), and *Vergil's "Aeneid" 8 and 11: Italy and Rome* (2006), and editor of *Brill's Companion to Ovid* (2002).

William Fitzgerald is University Lecturer in Classics and Fellow of Gonville and Caius College, Cambridge. He is the author of *Catullan Provocations* (1995), *Slavery and the Roman Literary Imagination* (2000), and *Martial: The Epigrammatic World* (forthcoming in 2007).

James M. May is Professor of Classics and Provost and Dean of the College at St. Olaf College, Northfield, Minnesota. He is the author of *Trials of Character: The Eloquence of Ciceronian Ethos* (1988), coauthor of *Thirty-Eight Latin Stories* (1986, 1995), coauthor of *Cicero: On the Ideal Orator* (2001), and editor of *Brill's Companion to Cicero: Oratory and Rhetoric* (2002).

Richard F. Thomas is Professor of Greek and Latin at Harvard University. He is the author of (most recently) *Virgil and the Augustan Reception* (2001), *Reading Virgil and his Texts* (1999), and coeditor of *Classics and the Uses of Reception* (2006). He is working on a commentary of Horace, Odes 4, and is coediting a book of essays on Bob Dylan's performance artistry.